Dr. Dennis Mulumba

I0462765

Real Estate Investing Mastery to Make millions

Table of Contents

COPYRIGHT

CHAPTER ONE

INTRODUCTION INVESTING IN YOUR FUTURE

Through real estate investing, many individuals just like you have been able to increase their net worth substantially, obtain the things they always wanted to have, reached their financial goals faster than they thought possible, and preserved their wealth for their retirement and/or their families. And many have done so without much money to start with, or without any money to start with at all.

The fact is real estate investing is a powerful tool for building and preserving wealth no matter where you live and no matter who you are. And, unlike some investment opportunities, real estate investing has "staying power."

Demand for real estate in most areas is constant although there are economic factors that influence the market and its demands. The good news is that when the economy is in a slump, there are tremendous opportunities for good real estate deals because the number of buyers decreases along with tougher economic times. Now, it is just such a time that makes investing in real estate more lucrative than ever. The key to building wealth through real estate is having the knowledge to understand the market swings and pressures and then being able to capitalize on the opportunities as you find them. There will always be an never-ending supply of buyers looking for everything from their first home to their retirement home—and you will be the investor who has exactly what these buyers need.

Before we go into greater detail in this manual about profiting with real estate, locating and negotiating deals, evaluating properties, and making the most out of some of real estate's best opportunities, let's take a brief look at the real estate investment market in general to see why it provides so many avenues for building wealth.

THE MAJOR BENEFITS
OF REAL ESTATE

The benefits of investing in real estate are many, from creating situations where your profit potential is up to you, to building a lifestyle some people only dream of. With real estate, you can:

• Own your own business Work part-time or full-time, be your own boss, and time things according to your schedule and goals.

• Take advantage of appreciation Real estate typically appreciates around four to five percent annually. This appreciation rate generally takes place as part of natural market growth, essentially, without you doing anything.

To illustrate, consider homeowners who purchased their homes 20 years ago and now find themselves with $150,000 in equity in their homes, something they never thought about at the time they purchased the home. Beyond that, you can create situations where you "force" appreciation, such as through renovations or cosmetic improvements to a home (we call this rehabbing properties). This is where the work you put into a property makes it instantly more valuable than the price you paid for it.

• Generate positive cash flow you can use – Some investors will purchase property in order to rent it out and create positive monthly cash flow. Property can sometimes be rented for more than the total expenses(principal and interest, taxes, and insurance), so you can make money from the rental, while someone else is building equity in your property. Another way to buy and hold property is to lease it to someone else with an option for them to purchase it in the future. This technique creates excellent positive monthly cash flow since these tenants are willing to pay more than the average renter will pay.

• Create a hedge against inflation – Even in times of inflation, opportunities abounds with the real estate. That's because inflation tends to force higher real estate prices and because the underlying asset (your property) can be counted on to be there through inflation (while some other investments may not survive economic downturns).

• Make money with low risk and low start up costs – The market for potential customers is huge and you can start your business in real estate investing with little or even no capital of your own. There are always private investors in the marketplace who have the money to invest but do not know how (or don't care to do the work) to do the deals themselves.

• Profit from equity buildup – You build equity at the same time as the property is naturally increasing in value due to market conditions and demand. And, you can tap that equity in a property, to finance additional investments.

• Enjoy multiple channels for profit – There are many ways to invest in real estate and there is something for everyone, from the casual or first-time investor to the more experienced or full-time investor. Once you understand the variety of opportunities available, you can choose the deals, that help you reach your individual goals faster.

• **Benefit from real estate's repeatability** – Once you learn the basics, learning advanced skills is even easier than you might realize. You can use the knowledge you build about real estate investing to repeat the process over and over again, on multiple types of properties, increasing your profits considerably without working harder to do so.

• **Benefit from tax breaks** – When you invest in real estate, consult with a tax professional about the opportunities that may be available to you through depreciation, in writing off certain business expenses, and through tax breaks (for example, deducting the interest portion of mortgage payments).

• **Finding investment properties and opportunities easily** – With real estate investing, opportunities are all around you. You can make a simple effort, like driving through neighborhoods looking for Sale By Owner signs, or you can do everything from establishing relationships with real estate professionals to placing your own ads to generate leads. What's nice to know is that regardless of the time you have available, there are many easy ways to find the opportunities that will help you succeed.

• **Market your business easily** Marketing real estate is not complicated. Everything from a For Sale sign in the front yard of a home you have renovated to an ad or direct mail campaign can bring customers. Some investors have netted thousands of dollars in profit on dealssimply because someone called them from a car magnet ad on the side of their vehicle or from a flyer they posted on a community bulletin board at an apartment complex.

• **Build a power team to help you increase and expedite your** profits – To succeed with real estate investing, you will want to establish solid relationships throughout your community like-minded investors and in the business... relationships with people who can help you build your business and succeed, partner with you in investments or deals, or be available to buy your properties. A winning team of contacts which would include people like a good real estate lawyer also called conveyancer in some countries, real estate agents or brokers, an accountant or/and a tax expert, a mortgage broker, a professional home inspector, letting Agent, insurance broker, a good bond originator, an architect, a town planner, real estate mentors or coaches who can guide you through transactions or deals and help motivate you as well as keep you accountable, and qualified contractors, builders, and other professionals who can assist you in rehabbing your properties.

• Help others – One great aspect of real estate investing is you can help others in need. Consider someone who has a distressed property because they live in another state and they're trying to manage it long distance. You could help alleviate that burden! Or consider someone who is struggling with debt and now the bank is going to foreclose on their home. You could help them save their credit. The possibilities for helping others are endless.

A MARKET FULL OF OPPORTUNITIES

There are not only many benefits associated with the real estate, but also many opportunities for success regardless of your financial goals, location, the financial situation, and what is more important is to get a good and knowledgeable real estate investment coach or mentors such as Dr. Dennis Mulumba or other experts in this field.

Short -term and long-term strategies

With real estate, there are both short-term and long-term investment strategies available to you, giving you the flexibility to make investment choices that fit your schedule and needs. As an example, you may wish to hold properties only for the short-term, so you might purchase a property below fair market value, fix it up with minor repairs and cosmetic improvements (such as painting and landscaping), and then turn around and sell it quickly for profit.

You can even purchase or contract for a distressed property at well below fair market value, and sell either the property or the right to buy the property, immediately to another investor who will do all the work improving the property. This short-term strategy is known as "quick-turning" or wholesaling properties.

Individuals have made fast profits of thousands of dollars on just one deal in wholesaling a property and you can too! Additionally, investors have used wholesaling strategies to make quick cash to pay down their debts, generate extra income in addition to a fulltime job, start their own business slowly and with limited risk, and create capital for future investments.

A long-term strategy might be to buy a home below fair market value and then rent it out for any number of years or lease it to someone else giving them an option to purchase it in the future. In situations like these, when you have tenants, they are building your equity because with every payment they make to you, you are taking that payment and decreasing your existing mortgage by paying some extra money every month toward the bank (s) capital. This, in turn, will reduce bank interest you are originally supposed to pay on your mortgage over the years.

The implication will also be that the numbers of years to pay back will be reduced, and this same strategy will be increasing your credit score sensibly.

Opportunities are in all areas and countries

You can make money with real estate regardless of the area you live or invest in. This book will begin helping you to become knowledgeable about how to analyze and identify profit potential in real estate markets. Your future training will take you to the next level and to those who are committed, the potential for wealth accumulation will be unlimited.

Just few examples of ways to build wealth follow and illustrate this point. For example, in low-income areas, you can find several great opportunities for rehabbing or wholesaling properties. These opportunities allow the owner/landlord to provide affordable, clean housing for low-income families, while generating positive cash flow through highly profitable weekly or monthly rentals. When you act as the intermediary investor, they provide a way to generate income through either quick turns after the rehab or fast cash through wholesale techniques.

In moderate-income areas or affordable housing, you can profit from excellent resale values and work with large market of first-time home buyers who may need special financing options to purchase their home. Moderate-income areas can also provide good rental income opportunities.

In just above median home value areas there are currently great prospects for two techniques: either offering lease options to potential homebuyers, or buying at substantial discounts due to distressed seller situations and then holding the properties for shortterm for profits at the time of sale.

And finally, there is tremendous opportunity in some of the best neighborhoods and school districts in the cities across the U. S. due to the distress of the sellers who must get out of a property quickly. While not for the beginning investor, these types of deals can give experienced investors the opportunity to invest when tax shelters are the priority.

Evaluating Buy & Hold Properties

If you intend to buy and hold property for cash flow, it is important that you learn to choose or locate properties that will cash flow—and the United States has an abundance of properties available that will meet your needs! Having said that, if you are considering rental housing, you need to consider carefully the benefits of buying houses that have more than one stream of income coming in each month. For example, if you are buying a single family house to rent out, if it is vacant for a month, you are making the entire mortgage payment. However, if instead of buying single family houses to rent out you focus on duplexes, triplexes, and quads, if one of the units is empty, you still have the other(s) to help cover your expenses. That is part of the beauty of real estate—various tweaks on your buying decisions can make big differences in the outcome of the deal. And in this scenario, the price of a duplex is seldom anywhere close to double the price of the single family. Yet, the rents from each unit are not half as much as the single family's rental income price. For that reason, it is unusual for us to recommend you buy and rent out single family homes in working class neighborhoods. Go for the duplex! On the other hand, in the upper income neighborhoods, lease options work beautifully on single family homes because you will be dealing with future buyers of the property from the beginning. Knowing what to buy, where to buy, and how to hold will move you to your financial dreams more quickly than you can imagine—the opportunities are endless!

MULTIPLE FINANCING OPTIONS

Real estate investing can be done virtually anywhere by anyone —the key is knowledge. It provides a way for any individual to get involved and reach their financial goals, regardless of their current financial situation. That's because there are many creative financing and buying approaches available. You just have to know where and how to look for them. For example, you can find opportunities through:

• **Government programs** – There are many ways to purchase homeswell below fair market value through government-sponsored programs, and there are ways to use government programs to find opportunities you could not find anywhere else.

• **Seller financing** – You can take advantage of seller financing, lease options, etc., to allow you to purchase properties with little or no money down.

• **Sources for seed money (capital) to finance your investment** – Even people with poor credit have still been able to achieve success in real estate investing; you just have to know how to look for the creative financing opportunities. Some examples include seller financing, wraparound mortgages, equity financing, partnering with other investors, etc.

So, for many reasons, real estate provides people with opportunities to profit and earn income in ways they never would have dreamed possible. The more you learn and the more prepared you are to take on new opportunities, the better you'll succeed in generating amazing profits and changing your life forever. We are dedicated to helping you get there.

CHAPTER TWO

The circle of wealth Multiple Streams of Income in Real Estate Investing

CREATING YOUR PERSONAL BUSINESS ROAD MAP

If you were going to travel from New York City to San Francisco, there are such good road signs and highways systems across the United States that you could probably find your way without having a detailed road map that outlined your journey. But doing so would not make much sense, would it? You would end up taking a few wrong turns, you'd have trouble getting started, and ultimately, you would be sure to get lost few times along the way. The same is true for choosing to invest in any business. Having a clear idea of the benefits and advantages of different types of real estate deals, clearly evaluating where you are in terms of resources, and moving in the right direction with the least amount of wasted time will be a tremendous asset to you. That is the purpose of this chapter—to help you begin to get more clear about where you are, where you want to go, and the best way to get there.

One of the first things you should do is a personal financial evaluation, of where you are at this moment in time. Do you have strong or weak credit? Do you have access to money lending sources? Are they public (lenders, banks, mortgage brokers) or private (personal contacts who might be willing to help you to get started)? Once you have clearly delineated your current position you are better able to begin choosing the right types of deals to move you towards financial freedom. For example, if you have few financial or credit resources, you will want to choose types of real estate deals (at least in the early stages of your career) that do not rely on either credit or funding. One of these types of deals is called "wholesaling." So, let's begin this chapter by outlining the various ways to make money—and the type of money it takes to do that kind of deal.

MANY PROPERTY TYPES AND INVESTMENT STRATEGIES

Real estate investing is attractive because there are many property types to invest in, as well as many strategies for what to do with those properties. And each comes with its own rewards. The following are some of the main types of investment opportunities, with their primary benefits listed.

Technique/ circumstance	Benefit
Wholesale buying & contract sales	Quick cash return/low cash investment
Lease Option	Cash flow, appreciation/ can be structured with a low cash investment
Foreclosure	Quick cash (short-term), needs some cash to do
Rehabbing	Quick cash, cash flow/needs cash or credit investment
Mobile Homes	Cash flow/low cash investment
Tax Liens & Deeds	Portfolio income from interest/ higher cash investment/little leverage
Property Management (Managing other investors' property)	Cash flow/ very low cash investment needed to begin

Investors consider different options based on the outcome they want to achieve, the amount of cash they want to invest in the project, and/or their level of experience with different strategies.

For example, an investor may want to consider quick cash investment strategies for a variety of reasons, among them being high consumer debt (generating quick cash to pay down that debt) or lack of seed capital to work with (using wholesale opportunities to quickly build more money for future investments). Of course, with multiple income streams and opportunities comes the need to obtain the proper knowledge to specialize in different areas. Because wholesaling, foreclosures, and lease options are some of the more popular ones in real estate investing, we have included chapters focused specifically on those strategies in this manual. This book also introduces you to several other streams of income in real estate investment and defines the types of income those strategies can produce. As you grow your business and find the real estate investment areas and strategies that interest you most, you can discuss with us more opportunities for advanced training in those areas so you can maximize your profit potential.

THE CIRCLE OF WEALTH AND MULTIPLE INCOME STREAMS

You might be wondering how to choose your streams of income and what factors should influence your decision, so before we go any deeper into this book, let's take some time to define the various types of income and the benefits of choosing one over the other.

Types of Earned Streams of Income in Real Estate:

• Wholesaling

• Foreclosures, Pre-foreclosures, and Real Estate Owned Properties (Postforeclosures)

• Rehabbing

• Probate

• Discount Note Selling

• Remodeling

• Land Development

Basically, anything that you are going to contract and sell

quickly would fall into the Earned Income category.

Passive Income: Passive income is money that comes to you week after week or month after month without you going out and doing another deal. This type of income is also sometimes called "recurring income." In real estate, these types would be your buy and hold properties—your rentals and leases. Once you have closed on these deals you can collect the rent (or your property manager collects it for you) every single month. Another real estate related field of income that would be considered passive is when you become a property manager, have a property management company, and investors hire you to collect the rents for them and pay you a fee for doing it on their behalf!

Types of passive Streams of Income in Real Estate:

• Rentals—houses, apartments, mobile homes, etc.

• Leases—lease option properties

• Property Management— mentioned above

• Recreational Parks— where you rent out spaces

• Mobile Home Parks— where you rent out lots and others own the mobile homes

• Apartment Houses— which bring you in multiple payments every month

•Commercial Spaces — offices, retail establishments, storage unit facilities, industrial buildings, etc...

Buy and hold properties are where you build long-term wealth and begin to benefit from appreciation and tax advantages. So, earned income streams help you generate the cash to move towards buying and hold long term wealth! The two work hand in hand to help you achieve your goals.

Portfolio Income: Portfolio income is when your money begins to make money for you—typically through interest. Let's say you have $30,000 to invest in some type of real estate related deal but you do not want to have to do any work or invest any time once you have made your purchase. In this situation, you might choose to invest that money in tax liens that earn a return of 18% per year. You attend the tax lien auction, purchase liens that take the $30,000 investment amount, and then you sit back and wait for them to be redeemed! Your money begins earning interest at the rate of 18% per year the day you pay for the liens and the county property tax office employee does all the monitoring and paperwork! That sure beats investing in a CD at 1% or 2% interest, doesn't it?

There are several other ways for you to generate portfolio income that is real estate related, as well. Most of these streams of income relates to the investor earning interest on his or her money. While this book will not go into depth on these techniques, it is important for you to at least understand the potential and definition of these income streams.

TYPES OF PORTFOLIO STREAMSOF INCOME IN REAL ESTATE:

- Tax Lien Auction Investments
- Discount Note Buying
- Seller Financing
- Hard Money Lending
- Venture Capital

In real estate, you will often hear others refer to "The Circle of Wealth." Real estate can allow investors to create wealth through a very systematic process that builds upon itself. Here's how it looks and how it works:

While everyone is different, with different goals and demands on their time, professional real estate investors will typically want to have three to five streams (and accompanying knowledge bases) of earned income, three to five streams of passive income, and two to three streams of portfolio income.

New investors who have a limited amount of money begin by becoming knowledgeable in few earned income streams such as wholesale, foreclosure, and rehabbing. Now they have more control over their ability to generate large amounts of cash in a short period of time. They then take that money and begin to invest in buy and hold properties such as lease option houses. They have now learned to invest safely, and once we learn to do it safely, we can do it quickly!

As the passive income grows or the lease option properties begin to sell (usually three years later), the investor has two choices: either buy another buy and hold property or invest in a portfolio stream (such as tax liens, defined above).

Begin to train your mind to think in terms of The Circle of Wealth and always ask yourself what your short and long term goals are at any given moment. Yes, we get rich in buy and hold situations, so that is your ultimate goal, but if you are beginning with limited resources and need to generate some cash so you can build a substantial portfolio in a fairly modest number of years, earned income can help you do that.

An Important Consideration: As investors, it is crucial for us to "begin with the end in mind." Now, I realize that you might be starting on a shoestring and you probably have immediate needs that you want real estate to assist you in fulfilling. However, this business can be one of the best ways for you to become a millionaire or a multi-millionaire—and on some level you understand that or you would not be reading this book. So, set aside your fear and discouragement from yesterday and ask yourself, "If I could retire in ten years and own and control 350 apartments in a good neighborhood that produced $25,000 per month in positive cash flow, would I feel safe and secure about my financial future and my golden years?" I believe that most of you would answer this question with a resounding, "Yes!"

So, let's begin your investing business with that level of commitment to your future.

The Circle of Wealth can help you achieve those goals. Consider it carefully and ask yourself what it could mean to your current lifestyle (and checkbook balance) if you had 7-10 streams of income and could generate both short and long term cash flow. Then, commit to your future, to your accumulation of knowledge, and to having a mentor or coach to guide you along the way.

AN INTRODUCTION TO SOME KEY AREAS OF REAL ESTATE INVESTMENT COVERED IN THIS BOOK

Before we delve deeper into these subjects, let's take a moment to discuss some of the key property and investment types in overview form to familiarize you with some of your options and prepare you for what you are about to learn from this material.

MAKING THE RIGHT INCOME STREAM CHOICES

Distressed Properties Vs. Distressed or Motivated Sellers

There is an old maxim when it comes to real estate investing: "There are only two types of deals out there—either distressed properties or distressed sellers." Regardless of your investment strategy or targeted property type, you will find that some properties provide more ideal investment opportunities than others. When we refer to a property as "ideal," we do so for a reason. The word is also an acronym for the following:

I = Income (Produces Cash Flow)

D =Depreciable (Offers Tax Advantages)

E =Equity (Equity Build-up Increase Net Worth)

A =Appreciation (Increases in Value)

L =Leverage (Increases Return on Investment)

As professional investors, we weigh each deal against the ideal and then consider the benefits of that type of deal versus another opportunity. We do not always hit each one of these characteristics—particularly in the beginning of our investment careers—but we always evaluate and make informed choices.

When considering a distressed property, we are looking for the following advantages:

• There is often less competition for them since the average individual wants properties in good condition.

• Most market areas offer numerous distressed properties to choose from.

• You can often purchase distressed properties under flexible, easy terms, and for prices substantially below market value, making for a nice profit margin on resale or good cash flow on the rental property.

• You have the ability to instantly increase your property's value through minor improvements and rehab work (forced appreciation).

Some things to think about with distressed properties include:

• Most real estate markets have a sizable number of investor's looking for these types of properties, so your marketing efforts need to be active, well planned, and effective to find good deals. It would be wise to investigate different marketing strategies that have worked well for other real estate investors, and to find others in the business that are willing to teach you where to look for opportunities and provide tips on how to bring opportunities to you.

• To avoid costly mistakes, you'll need to know how to effectively evaluate the property and its neighborhood.

• Thorough inspections and repair estimates should be performed prior to a purchase.

• If the property is in a lower income and/or older neighborhood, the comparable sales in that area will not go over a certain amount of money, no matter how much improvement is made. Repairs are often costly—so in order to maximize profitability in the older, lower income areas, it is typically safer to combine a distressed property with a distressed seller and maximize the profit potential on each aspect.

Advantages of working with distressed sellers include:

• There is seller distress in every price range.

• You can sometimes purchase properties under flexible and easy terms. The seller needs help and, in many cases, just needs a way out, but does not know what to do. You can provide the solution.

• Seller distress is often caused by property distressed; so the chances of being able to increase property value through cosmetic improvements or rehabbing when you can match a distressed seller with a distressed property are excellent.

Things to think about with distressed sellers include:

• Seller distress must be handled delicately. These sellers are going through rough personal, professional, or financial times and they can be experiencing all kinds of emotions.

• You must know what put the seller in the situation they are currently in and figure out the best way to help them get out of it. In order to understand their problem and solve it, you will need to develop good listening and negotiating skills.

• Some distressed sellers present compelling reasons why they want to stay in their properties and the tendency is to want to accommodate this. If their challenge is for financial reasons, this can be risky. The saying goes that it is important to keep your emotions out of it.

WHOLESALE BUYING

Distressed properties make for a great wholesaling candidates. And wholesaling is an excellent opportunity because it requires little expertise and typifies the quick cash type of deal that many beginning investors are looking for.

Wholesale deals may be one of the first types of deals you will make in real estate investing because it's easy to identify distressed properties and there is such great potential for quick cash.

To truly be successful with wholesaling, some of the things you will need to learn include how to: properly segment your market; develop a database of potential properties, investors, and buyers; understand the multiple ways to target and market for wholesale deals; locate absentee owners; build a network with other investors; and develop key strategies that will help you close deals.

In addition, you should master several basic aspects of the wholesaling business, including:

Prescreening prospects – Since distressed properties should be your primary target, you should learn how to both identify and evaluate distressed properties. You should also understand that a distressed property does not necessarily mean a deal is good, but that it is a good start. So you need to master the techniques to know when a deal is too good to be true, when it's time to move forward, and when the deal needs to be left on the table. It will also help to know how to identify a motivated seller, because the combination of a motivated seller and a distressed property will make this opportunity far more advantageous.

Determining market value – You need to understand the importance of determining fair market value after repairs to be a successful wholesaler. The real estate professionals on your power team will be key assets for getting this information. Also, using comparable sales of homes in the same market area will help you determine fair market value.

Estimating repairs – This won't be a successful venture if you do not estimate repairs correctly. Learn how to analyze deals to ensure you make an offer that will result in the most profit. There are also strategies you can learn that will save you money on rehab projects and maximize your profits.

Making offers and counteroffers – You need to become familiar with good negotiating and communication skills, learn how to make offers and counteroffers effectively without compromising your goals, and learn how to work with contracts. Knowing how to properly evaluate properties will be critical to determining not only what to offer, but if you should make an offer at all.

Lining up buyers – Wholesaling is actually only partially complete if you can find and negotiate deals, but you have nobody lined up to readily assign contracts to. Building a sizable investor database to tap regardless of the type of deal you are working on will help you move things forward quickly and preserve your profit margins.

Closing effectively – You need to learn the strategies necessary to close without cash, including how to do contract assignments and simultaneous closings.

LEASE OPTIONS

Lease options represent one of the most attractive real estate investment opportunities for both new and experienced investors particularly because they can generate multiple streams of income within a single deal. The following offers a few general points about using lease options to invest in real estate:

If you buy a property with lease option, you can:

• Gain control of a property without taking ownership of the property – You have no obligation to buy, but you have established the right to buy.

• Work with distressed sellers, not with distressed properties – Seller circumstances create the deal. What you need to do is find the problem owners.

• Live in or control nice homes in nice areas – In these cases, the seller needs to get out and investors want to get in (an excellent match!). Desirable neighborhoods create demand.

• Help someone else in many cases – The determining factor in lease options is often debt relief. You are usually working with people who may not necessarily want to sell their property, but who must sell it because of financial problems. You can help someone else reach a solution quickly. Meanwhile, you can do it with little or no money out of-pocket.

If you sell property with lease option, you can:

• Benefit from large market of motivated buyers – Lease options can be very attractive to people who are just starting out or who are starting over. And lease options may be the only option available to some people based on their credit circumstances.

• Find multiple profit centers through lease options – You can create positive monthly cash flow for yourself, collect a non-refundable option consideration, and profit from the difference between what you paid for the property and what price you set for your tenant/buyer.

FORECLOSURES

The foreclosure market can also provide a great avenue for profit for the beginning to experienced investor. Foreclosures, while unfortunate, are an everyday occurrence, and this can be your opportunity to not only make a wise investment, but also to help someone in need. Remember that foreclosures can happen for any number of reasons, and this is an area where you can really create a win-win situation and do something that benefits both you and the person who might be in trouble. Investors must be able to effectively negotiate with both lenders and homeowners to optimize profits on these deals.

IT'S-A LEARNING PROCESS

With so many strategies to employ and ways to make money in real estate, knowledge will be key to your success.

By investigating the opportunities available in real estate investing, you have taken your first important step towards obtaining financial independence. Now, it's time to move on to the next level with the guidance and knowledge you can receive through our program and this manual. Every part of this program has been designed to help you achieve increasing levels ofknowledge and success as a real estate

investor.

You'll soon see that, with the material presented here, you can easily learn how to spot distressed properties, motivated sellers, and opportunities that will afford you the most profit. You can learn how to line up investors before you buy properties to limit your risk and how to line up potential buyers before you move forward on deals. You can become adept at finding motivated sellers simply by knowing what to look for in their ads and more successful with your sales simply by knowing what to write in yours. You can learn how to rehab properties to maximize profits with minimal investment, including what to look for and what to avoid, as well as how to make money by wholesaling properties without ever having to fix them up. And you can master the negotiating strategies necessary to get the best deal or know when to walk away from the table.

CHAPTER THREE

UNDERSTANDING MARKET ANALYSIS & EVALUATION

Investing Is About Supply and Demand: One of the most important things you can learn when it comes to real estate investing is market analysis—having the ability to evaluate a market, whether your own or one in another part of the United States, and determine if the values are going up, going down, or are flat. This is where amateur investors fall short in their knowledge and this lack of understanding creates problems for them when they buy, hold, and sell.

HISTORY IS A GREAT TEACHER— AND PREDICTOR OF THE FUTURE:

A little bit of history from the past ten years will illustrate our points as we begin to increase our understanding of market analysis. In 2000, the stock market was in a self-correction process and investors who typically put their money in stock were worried about their earnings and profit potential in the short term. In any investment, there will be periodic self-corrections in a market, whether it is real estate, stock, or even in gold. Prices and values go up, they hit a peak, they stabilize, and if they are not in line with what the market will bear, they will go back down until they reach the point that buyers will once again make purchases.

To add to the situation with stock investments, in late 2001 us Americans experienced the trauma of September 11th and there was more emotional fear which was generated by this event than our population has seen on a collective level and in our entire lifetimes and history. The natural reaction of people in the grips of uncertainty is to do nothing—to "batten down the hatches" until the storm is over. Note that this is not an investor reaction because a storm means more opportunities available, in our opinion. The problem with this reaction is the paper currency that we operate on in the United States. The way our economy flourishes is for the paper to keep moving. When the flow of money stops, the economy stalls.

To encourage the American people to buy/spend their money and keep the paper moving, the Federal Reserve dropped interest rates—which allowed people to buy property with far less interest expense than historic levels had demanded. Additionally, loan programs were rolled out with much more lenient lending guidelines so many more people were able to qualify for loans than historic guidelines in the past had provided.

So, with the stock market in a state of stagnation or self-correction, average home interest rates lower than they had been in over thirty years, and lending guidelines more lenient than we had seen in decades, people began to take their accessible investment money and purchase homes and land.

In essence, we had a "blue light special" or buying frenzy kick into full gear and real estate became the investment strategy of choice for many people who had never owned real estate, at all! Adding to that, investors who were disillusioned with the performance of the stock market began pulling available revenue from this type of investing and move it to real estate.

On top of the stimulus of low interest rates and extremely relaxed lending qualifications, the first waves of baby-boomers were within few years of retiring. As they saw the opportunity to invest (and also saw the non-performance of their stock portfolios), they began visiting retirement states and purchasing their homes or condominiums earlier than they had planned. This was typically a wise move on their part—but it created an increased demand on real estate that was unexpected. When opportunities to make money abound, builders will rise to the occasion.

Since there were not enough houses available to purchase, pre-construction plans became the norm. The mantra across the United States became, "Pay a 20% non-refundable deposit, contract for us to build a home or condo at a pre-agreed upon price, and when construction is complete, you can close." That accomplished two different things: people were working (construction picked up dramatically, jobs were in abundance, and building materials were flying off the shelves), and paper was moving! For the potential investor, a feeling of "locking in a price" was of utmost importance. If the investor was "buying" in a 20% appreciation rate market, and if the condo was going to take two years to complete, life seemed golden! The condo would theoretically be worth 40% more upon completion (and closing) that the contract price! Talk about getting rich quick— it sure felt as if the goose was laying a golden basket of eggs!

However, depending upon where an investor was in the market cycle of self-correction, was there going to be a buyer for the property to do a quick turn? In 2002, the answer was a resounding, "You Betcha'!" However, by 2005 and 2006, the buyers had exhausted their buying ability (run out of money) and the markets began to stall.

Since real estate revolves around supply and demand, if there are not buyers that match sellers, the market will stall—which is what happened. What a concept—ultimately, there must be someone to live in a house or condo once it is built.

HOW DOES THAT RELATE TO TODAY'S MARKETS?

The following diagram provides a graphic view of what happened, where we are right now, and what to expect based upon historical data, in the future. The solid diagonal line (A) indicates where we should have been in terms of appreciation. The vertical line (B) in 2002-05 shows what happens when demand skyrockets. The declining line (C) illustrates what is happening across much of the country as prices self-correct to get back to the markets' "normal" line of appreciation.

Do you notice that when we have an upward self-correction, the prices will tend to rise too high and too fast for the market to bear (for a period of time) and then come down too much and too fast on the downward side? That is due to the tendency for people to live and make decisions based upon recency bias! If everyone else is buying, they hear about it, jump on the band wagon, and they buy! If everyone else is afraid to buy, they jump on the band wagon, and they are afraid to buy! Warren Buffet has a saying that comes to mind in these situations, and to paraphrase him, it comes down to, "When everyone else is greedy, be afraid. When everyone

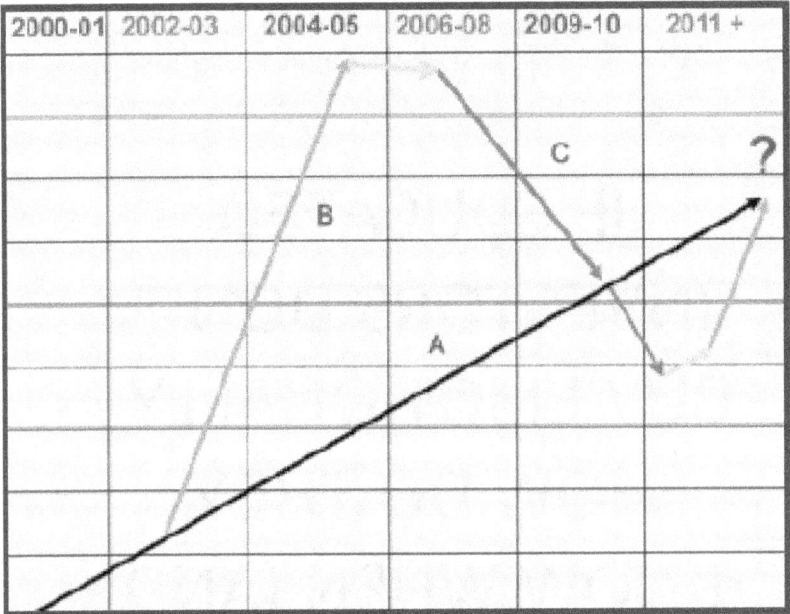

2000-01	2002-03	2004-05	2006-08	2009-10	2011 +

else is afraid, be greedy." In essence, the professional investor will typically do the opposite of what the general population of amateur investors is doing.

It is a good habit not to conform yourself to things or the general understanding without asking questions and investigating the why question. Question of the mindset, this mindset of the why is the mother of all inventions over the course of human history.

IF EDUCATED INVESTORS DON'T BUY EMOTIONALLY, HOW DO THEY KNOW WHEN (AND WHERE) TO BUY?

Several factors in real estate drive real estate prices. For example (and this is simply common sense), if a market has high unemployment rates, the local economic conditions are dismal, and interest rates are high, the real estate market will stall along with sales of other goods and services

Let's take a moment and list the factors that influence and drive the real estate market and prices:

- Interest rates & inflation
- Lending qualifications
- A vailability of housing
- Tourism
- Job growth and stability

- Industry & Manufacturing

- Population growth

- Demographic changes

Every city has historic numbers for appreciation rates—how much per year, on a fairly long-term basis, the value of real estate increased, on average.

In most areas of the country, real estate goes up approximately 4-5% per year. Now, some years there may be little change in prices, and then in other years there will be a jump to correct the lack of growth in previous years—but when we take a 25 year average of the median home prices, we see what the city's average growth has been in percentage points. That percentage tells us what to expect for a area's overall growth rate, prior to factoring in anomalies such as an new factory moving into the area that brings in thousands of new jobs.

So now we have an annual average and can base our decisions and projections for appreciation on numbers, rather than feelings. This is a key point! Human beings who are not knowledgeable about a topic tend to make decisions on an emotional level —and then to compound the problem, they have what I refer to as "recency bias." Whatever is happening today, sure feels as if it will always be happening. That is not a good place to make decisions from! Think about this for few minutes—if real estate is dramatically increasing in value at a rapid rate, it sure feels as if you'd better jump on the bandwagon and buy real estate in that area!

This is what happened to many investors between 2003 and 2006. The news came on at 6 p.m. and the announcer conveyed the new NAR (National Association of Realtors) Quarterly appreciation rates for the largest 125 cities in the country and Bradenton/Sarasota, FL. was #1 in the nation! What did uneducated investors do? They jumped on an airplane for Bradenton and bought four houses—and they had no understanding of the above factors that influence demand on real estate in the long term scheme of things!

YOU'VE GOT TO KNOW WHEN TO HOLD—AND WHEN TO FOLD!

What was wrong with that picture? They bought AFTER the market had emerged and grown—not before or during the changes. What should they have done? A knowledgeable investor would have been researching markets for areas that were under-valued prior to the drop in interest rates and lending qualifications. Then, the investor could target areas based upon his or her knowledge of the upcoming babyboomers who would be moving into certain areas of the country when they retired. And finally, the investor would have worked closely with professionals in that area and found out how many homes were on the market, how long listings were taking to move, and if any changes were taking place within the community to signal a change in expectations for that market.

So, a savvy investor in an under-valued city like Miami, just an example, would have been buying property in 2002, 2003, and 2004, but would have seen that prices were no longer in line with the economy of that city by early in 2004 and begun to sell before things got out of control in terms of the price of houses. Always remember, houses in any city are there for people to actually live in (what a concept)! If the average person does not make enough to live in a house or apartment (either buy or rent), there are going to be vacancies! Real estate is like a finely tuned instrument—it will self-correct or "retune" itself whenever the prices get too far out of line with the economy of the area.

The educated and knowledgeable investor would have been selling by 2004 and 2005—not buying! And, the people he or she would have been selling to would, in large part, have been the people who were buying airplane tickets and flying into the area to buy property that they didn't have the correct knowledge to buy.

WHAT THIS MEANS
TO YOU

At this point, you might ask yourself, "How do I find undervalued areas to invest in? How do I evaluate where those areas are in terms of the market cycle?" One of the best things you can do as you begin your real estate investing business is have a mentor to guide you through the process. He or she will know and understand the intricacies of investing and market analysis. As well, your mentor will work with you to identify new market trends that are taking place in the area under investigation, the number of days on market, the sub-areas within the overall city that are most likely to appreciate the most quickly, and those that are most likely to stall and begin self-correcting first.

Now, in a market that is already stalled, where do investors begin? Start by identifying the sub-neighborhoods that are moving the most quickly! Working with your real estate professional, do a zip code search for the areas that have the properties that are moving with the most frequency. And then, begin looking for distressed sellers that are highly motivated to sell in those zip codes. If one of your streams of income is going to be foreclosures, you could target all sellers within a certain zip code who are in pre-foreclosure status. If one of your investment strategies is to buy and hold using lease option techniques, you could then buy the pre-foreclosure, hold it for three years using lease option technique, and realize the benefits of the appreciation that the city's otherwise stalled market is not experiencing.

The key concept in this chapter is for new investors to understand the magnitude of analyzing a real estate market prior to buying property. If you are buying in a stalled real estate area, and you understand that, from the beginning, you will know to buy at large discount to cover and build in the lack of appreciation that you understand is going to be a part of that deal.

If you know where you are in a market cycle, you can buy, hold, or sell accordingly, as well as change or modify your exit strategy to complement the part of the cycleyou are in. The cycles or conditions of a real market are as follows:

Appreciating Markets: Areas where there is not enough housing, high demand, or a shortage of land. Areas where an increase in population is placing pressure on the housing market. Neighborhoods that are in high demand due to location, school districts or other influences are cause the area to be considered "choice."

Flat Markets: Areas that have a adequate amount of housing for the population and housing demands. Areas that have an abundance of land for future development and few restrictions on building new houses.

Self-Correcting Markets: Areas that have either gone up too quickly or too much due to dabblers investing and creating artificial demand that was not filled by actual long term buyers or tenants, or areas that are undervalued that need to adjust upward to change the pricing for that physical location's proximity to nearby, higher priced areas.

Depreciating Markets: Areas where industry, manufacturing, or tourism has declined, decreasing the demand on the existing available housing and new structures or sources of revenue are not yet in place to create an new demand.

Based on upon these definitions and categories of markets, where would you categorize your city, overall?

Many new investors, as they, evaluate their local markets, believe that property is depreciating when it is actually self-correcting. As well, they buy based upon price, rather than buying based upon market potential. Most new investors lean towards buying in the low or middle income areas because they feel the risk is lower. However, when market analysis is a part of your knowledge base, buying decisions are made based upon exit and holding strategies, not on fear of risk (bigger numbers).

CHAPTER FOUR

GETTING TO KNOW
YOUR MARKET

As we learned in the previous chapter, real estate investors must know how to analyze a overall market to determine what is happening within it at any given time. In addition, they must use their knowledge to identify the most profitable neighborhoods within that market for their various streams of income. Now, with that knowledge, we, can begin to look at ways to make wise buying decisions in the right places.

The most important thing you will do in real estate investing is to buy right (in other words, make the best deal possible when buying a property). This is where you will really make your money in real estate. In fact, you may have heard people say it before: you make your money when you buy; you just realize it when you sell your property and make a profit, or when you start getting positive cash flow from an income-producing property. And it's true. So, it's imperative you buy right, meaning you never pay too much for a property.

To do this, you need to get to know and understand the market you're buying in. After all, the only way you can calculate the after-repair value of a property is by knowing the fair market value of houses in the area you choose to concentrate in. It is a crucial part of the evaluation process.

TRUE MARKET VALUE

Some people think the true market value is what they see advertised in the classified section of the newspaper or in flyers they have pulled out of a box on real estate agent's sign. But that is a "wish list" – what the seller hopes to get. The true market value is not what people are asking for. It is what someone is willing to pay and someone else is willing to accept. And more specifically, it is the sales prices of houses that have sold within the last six months (not what they were listed for, but what they actually sold for).

No matter what type of real estate investing you do (buy, fix, and sell; wholesale; foreclosure; lease option; income property; etc.), you will need to understand your market. Understanding your market will help you know what to offer, how to recognize a good deal when you see one, and how to act quickly. And as you develop your knowledge of the market, you will be spending less time looking at properties that aren't worthwhile investments.

DEFINING THE AREA
YOU WILL INVEST IN

Start by looking in a low- to moderate-income neighborhood, where you will find a large inventory of properties. If you want to buy, fix, and sell, look for decent neighborhoods where it is clear neighbors care about their property and the community (these are often termed "We Care" neighborhoods).

If you want to wholesale properties (quick-turn properties to other investors – a popular and profitable strategy you will learn about in greater detail later), you will be looking more toward extremely distressed properties or neighborhoods.

Of course, in order to define your target area in relation to your goals, you need to know where each of these areas is in your city. If you are not sure where these areas are, you will need to segment your city with the help of your real estate agent. If you do not already have a real estate professional or need to know what to look for in a good real estate agent, please refer to Chapter Two.

SEGMENTING
YOUR AREA

Ask the real estate professional what the average price of a three bedroom, two bath, single family home is in your city. You also wants the agent to pull up a one-line MLS (multiple listing service) lists of single family homes. Sometimes they call this a "short form." Have the agent start at $0 and go to 120% of the average home price. With this information, you can now identify which areas are low-income, working class, middle-income, and higher-income neighborhoods. Next, take the average price of a home in your city and multiply it by 70% and by 110%.

For example:

$100,000 = average price

70% = $70,000

110% = $110,000

EXAMPLE				
Below 70% of Average	70% of Average	Average Home Price	110% of Average	110%+ of Average
Low Income Neighborhood	Working Class Neighborhood		Working Class Neighborhood	Middle Income Neighborhood
$70,000	$70,000	$100,000	$110,000	$110,000

Once you have this information, you will need to get a map of your city, which you can usually obtain directly from your city, purchase from a store, or find on the Internet. You will need to make at least two copies of this map. Have one copy enlarged to a size that allows you to easily see the streets and get this copy laminated. If you live in a large city, begin by concentrating on about a one-mile square area or on a 20 to 40-block square; you can gradually expand your area.

The second map should be on an 8 ½ x 11 inch sheet of paper that you can put in a notebook and carry with you in the car (you may need to use several sheets, depending on the size of your city). Write on the map where the low-income, working class, and the middle-income areas are based upon the information you received from the agent. Identify extremely distressed neighborhoods more appropriate for wholesaling opportunities. If you don't know where this areas are, talk to someone who is knowledgeable about your area. You can contact property management companies, appraisers, postal carriers, cable workers, or your local police. These maps will also help you understand what homes are selling for in different segments of your city. (Below are what was included in the map but the map could not fit-to-size following is the list thereof)

My City:

- Lease Options
- Apartments
- Wholesale
- Pre-closures
- Mobile Home Lease Options
- Pre-foreclosure Dovetailed with Buy & Hold Lease Options
- Rehab Potential: Revitalising Areas: Historic Grant & Tax Credits
- Commercial Office Space.

-    Land or New Development

As you become more familiar with real estate investing and the skills needed for the streams of income you will focus on, this map will become more valuable to you as time passes. Now, when you are searching the MLS list for various properties that are for sale, you can do specific searches of zip codes or neighborhoods when you are ready to go after your next lease option, foreclosure, wholesale, or rehab property.

DECIDE WHAT AREA YOU WANT TO FOCUS ON

As discussed before, pick an area you want to focus on. Your target area will depend on what kind of investing you want to do. For example, if you plan to buy a house, fix it up, and then resell it, you will be looking in the working to middle-income areas. If you want to do quick-turns without ever fixing up the property, you'll look in areas that are more distressed—areas that the rehabbers tend to work in. If you are not sure which area to target, then start with the working to middle-income neighborhoods. You can always expand to other areas later.

 nce you have completed this assignment, you will be able to go into another region, anywhere in the country, and get to know the market there quickly.

DETERMINING PROPERT Y VALUES USING COMPS

Now that you have picked your target area, you are ready to get to know the market. You will now ask the real estate agent to pull up the comps (nickname for comparables) within a certain neighborhood. What you will get is a list of properties that have sold within the last six months in the particular area where you are focusing your investing. The reason you need the agent to do this is because the comps help you understand the market. Earlier, we mentioned some people think the true market is what they see in the houses for sale section of the newspaper. But the true market is what someone is willing to pay and someone else is willing to accept in a competitive and open market.

Real estate appraisers use the sales comparison approach to identify properties that have recently sold that are similar in square footage, number of bedrooms, location, property type, available amenities, condition, etc. to the house, they are appraising. Appraisers will usually look at three houses and determine the value of the house they are appraising based upon the recent sales prices for those similar houses. Appraisers also look at other methods to determine the value of a property, such as a cost replacement method. With this method, they are comparing this house to what it would cost per square foot to build a new one. This method is not as accurate because supply and demand, as well as the economics for an area determines what people are willing to pay. You will find the appraised value leans heavily on the comparables

If you are buying rental properties, the appraiser will use an income approach. The value of the property is based upon the income it produces. This method is used in determining the value of multi-units.

Have the real estate agent pull up a list of houses that have sold within the last six months in the area you are focusing on. Ask the agent to pull up about 20 houses. If 20 houses haven't sold, that's okay. You can't make more houses sell than have sold. On the other hand, if the agent pulls up 40 houses, that's too many. Ask your agent to condense the list down either by square footage, number of bedrooms, geography, or style until you have 20 houses.

Keep in mind that information about houses that have sold within the last three months is more valuable than the comps that are six months old, since the market can change quickly.

WHAT THE COMPARABLES WILL TELL YOU

Looking at the list of properties that have sold within the last six months, you will see information about each house, such as:

Listed price – This is the price the house was listed for (the asking price).

Sold price – This is the price the house actually sold for.

Now you will know if the sellers got the price they were asking for or less.

Days on the market, or DOM – The number of days listed next to this tells you how many days the home stayed on the market before it was sold. Sometimes you will just see a number indicating the number of days it took to sell the property; other times, you may see both a listed and a sold date. Either way, this provides valuable information because it helps you understand the time it typically takes to sell a house in your area.

Square footage – This tells you the size of the house. It also helps you determine the cost per square foot that homes are selling for (some comps will actually list the price per square foot).

How many bedrooms and baths

Lot size – It may tell you the dimensions of the lot or indicate what percent of an acre the lot is (for example, .20 = one fifth of a acre).

Year built or age of house – This will either tell you the year the house was built or how old the house is.

This is the minimum information you should have on each of the comps. However, you will probably see more because you are going to ask the agent to include the remarks (or comments) and a picture. The reason the remarks are so valuable is you will be trying to figure out why these houses sold for the price they sold for. You will be driving by each of them, but because they have been sold, you will not be able to see inside. Since you cannot judge a house by its cover any more than you can judge a book by its cover, the remarks will give you a clue as to the condition of the house.

Things you may see in the remark section of the MLS include:

• Great Fixer-Upper

• Handyman Special

• Needs TLC

• Sold As-Is

Reading this, you will know the house probably needed some work even if it looks great on the outside.

Other things you may notice in the remarks

section are:

- Motivated Seller

- Must Sell

- Foreclosure

- Bank Owned

- Illness Forces Sale

- Divorce

- Transferred

When you see words like that, it could be an indicator the seller is motivated.

Drive By The Houses That Have Sold

When you get your comparables list, you need to drive by each of the houses on it. Stop the car and look out the window. Write down what you see. This is not a test to find something wrong with the property. The house may look great! You are just trying to figure out why the house sold for that price.

Start With The Roof

How does the roof look? You don't have to be a roofing expert to know it needs work if you see some missing shingles or shingles that are curling up.

Look At The Exterior Of The House

How does it look? Does it need work? Again, this is not a test to find what's wrong with the house. You have permission to write down, "House looks great." But if you do notice something is wrong, then write it down. Be sure to pay attention to the picture on the MLS sheet. If the picture does not look as nice as the house does now, then the person who bought the house probably fixed it up.

Look at the yard

Now, check out the yard. How does it look? Does it look groomed and taken care of? Again, pay attention to the picture.

CHAPTER FIVE

SELECTING A POWER TEAM

In order to be successful, you will need to work with others... people who know this business or can help you build yours, people who can help direct you to buyers for your properties or provide financial assistance, etc.

As an investor, you'll learn how to leverage your money, but you will also need to learn how to leverage your time. Careful selection of qualified people who can assist you in growing your business can help you manage your time and energy more effectively. And leveraging your team members' knowledge can also help you avoid making mistakes.

To help get you started, this chapter will introduce you to the key contacts you will most likely have on your power team. The important thing to remember is you don't need to try to do all the work yourself. Seek professional help and support and recognize you will need to learn to delegate certain responsibilities at some point.

You will find that putting your team together is an ongoing process. Your team will grow as you expand your knowledge of real estate and take advantage of additional income streams and opportunities.

FINDING THE RIGHT REAL ESTATE PROFESSIONAL

A good working relationship with a real estate professional is one of the most important assets an investor can have. For one, when a property you are interested in purchasing is listed with an agent you will want to have your own agent working with you to represent your best interests in the deal. Secondly, real estate professionals can help you evaluate deals by pulling up sold properties comparable to the one you are thinking of buying, giving you a good idea of the market value for that neighborhood. And third, Realtors have access to the Multiple Listing Service (MLS) remarks section, a valuable source for finding potential deals. The MLS is a cooperative exchange of listing information. When a seller lists his or her home with Realtors®, the listing is put on the MLS, making the home available for any agent who belongs to the MLS to bring a buyer and share in the commission with the listing agent.

The properties on the MLS will usually include pictures and a good deal of information about the property, including the address of the property, the number of bedrooms and baths, the square footage, and available amenities. The MLS may also include any special terms the seller may consider.

As we discussed in the previous chapter, the remark section of the listing will contain clues about the condition of the property and the motivation of the seller. Your agent can put keywords into the remark section to pull up properties of interest to you.

CHOOSING A REAL ESTATE PROFESSIONAL

When choosing an agent, you want someone who works in the business full time and has strong knowledge of his or her field.

You are looking for an agent who is creative, hard working, and aggressive, and who knows how and where to find deals. Most real estate professionals have not worked with investors and have never introduced themselves to the game of property investments. No, go with such! They have never done a creative transaction. This can be a challenge for you and it can take some time to find the right agent, but the time you spend will be well worth it. Since your agent is one of the most important, if not the most important, member of your power team, he or she cannot be your weakest link in your power team chain!

One of the most important things you are looking for is, an agent who thinks like you do—like a millionaire real estate wealth builder! Most agents are not receptive to "unusual" offers. They may not believe in "nothing down" offers or creative approaches. If you plan to make a creative offer and you are working with an agent who doesn't think "outside the box," it's time to find a right and an new one! In the meantime, insist on being the one to present the offer because you want the owner to hear the benefits of your offer. Believing in those benefits will be key to making a convincing presentation.

Tell the agent what you're looking for—and be specific. If you are beginning with wholesale deals, let the agent know you are looking for distressed properties that need repair. Do not let the agent pre-qualify you. Let them know you use private funding and can close quickly.

Find a real estate professional who works in your target area by driving through the neighborhood. Look for agent signs and pick the three companies with the most signs. As you do this, you may notice an agent dominating the area. Real estate agents usually "farm" an area, meaning they focus on a particular area and work it to get listings. They do this by actively contacting the owners through phone calls, mailing promotional material, and knocking on doors.

Begin your interview by saying, "We are real estate investors and we're buying houses in this area. We are looking for properties that are 20-30% below market and/or distressed properties in need of repair. We also look mainly for properties in need of cosmetic repairs. We are also looking for an agent who specializes in income properties such as apartment buildings, duplexes, and fourplexes. Is there someone in your office who fits that description?"

NOT TOO BIG,
NOT TOO SMALL,
JUST RIGHT!

One of the questions new investors have when it comes to choosing the right person to work with is, "How much experience should the agent have?" There is no one size fits all answer to this, but experience has shown me that somewhere between three and five years seems to be a good blend of knowledge about the business and not being too set in their ways.

REAL ESTATE PROFESSIONAL INTERVIEW SCRIPT

The following is a sample script of what you might say when interviewing potential agents.

"Hello, my name is _____. I'm in a position to do some investing in real estate. I am looking to buy properties in your area and I want to develop a relationship with someone who understands my needs.

I'm looking for any property that makes sense. I will consider everything: single family, and multi-units with a good cash flow. I'm interested in properties that are cosmetically distressed. Fixer-uppers are great. You know, paint, carpet, and a little cleanup, that sort of thing. I am not looking for any major repairs like plumbing or structural.

I can pay cash in some instances. Generally, I use private funding to purchase these houses and can close quickly (they think commission!). However, I am always interested in seller financing.

I am looking for an agent who will research the MLS for me to find properties that meet my criteria and fax or email me a copy of those listings. I will do a drive by and present offers on properties that I'm interested in.

This will be a good opportunity for both of us to make some money.

Are you able to help me out?"

• How long have you been in the real estate business? (You wants a minimum of three years of experience.)

• Do you specialize in any type of real estate? (Their specialty should preferably be your area of interest.)

• Do you specialize in any area of town?

• Do you have any satisfied customers I can talk to?

• Do you make real estate your living? (Answer should be yes!)

• Are you willing to put the time in to help me find the right properties?

• What neighborhoods are turning around properties more quickly than others?

• Do you have any banking connections? (Mortgage brokers, lenders, etc.)

• Can you recommend a good closing agent in town?

• How much is your commission?

• Do you have the flexibility to work with your broker?

• Is this a good time to buy? Why?

• What is your opinion of the direction the real estate market is headed?

• What are the average number of days on market in _____ zip code?

• Do you own any real estate in town? (You want this answer to be yes.)

• Have you ever owned investment property?

• Are there any areas you feel particularly good about? If so, why?

• Where would you invest if you were going to buy property yourself?

• What kind of properties would you buy?

• Does your firm manage properties? If yes, what do you charge?

• What is the vacancy rate in the area?

• How many properties do you have listed? (This is just to give you an idea of whether this agent works primarily as a buyer's or a seller's agent.)

• How many properties did you sell last year? (You want to see how busy they are.)

• Do you work with investors? If so, how many are you actively seeking properties for, right now?

• Are you available on the weekends?

• Do you have any properties for sale that would be a good investment for me?

• Are there any areas that seem to be going up in value faster than others? If they answer yes to this question, ask more questions —such as what is driving that market, why the demand is higher in this area, etc.

FINDING THE RIGHT MORTGAGE BROKER

A good mortgage broker can be the real estate investor's best friend. You want a broker who can put the deal together and get it closed.

Sometimes you have to go through several brokers until you find the one you want to work with, but remember that it never hurts to have more than one contact. In fact, we suggest that you have not one, but THREE, mortgage brokers on your team. Why? This keeps them on their toes and provides you with more loan products to choose from.

You are looking for a broker who has been in the business a while. You want one who is experienced in working with investors and bridge financing (hard money lenders). And you want one who is thoroughly familiar with FHA financing, local down payment assistance programs, grants, and hard money lending.

A mortgage broker or bond originator in some countries can be a good source for finding investment deals and is usually more creative than a banker when it comes to funding your opportunities.

When you talk with mortgage brokers, do not let them run a credit check until you find a creative mortgage broker you like. Every time they run a credit check, it can lower your score, so don't authorize a pre-approval credit check. The best way to find a good mortgage broker is often through a real estate professional. Interview at least five mortgage brokers before choosing the ones you will eventually work with.

Another good question to ask potential brokers is how they are creatively dealing with the tight lending policies in place at the present time. Find out what they will need you to have in terms of credit scores, down payments, and other qualifications in order to get deals closed.

MORTGAGE BROKER INTERVIEW

Ask the following questions to help determine if this is the right mortgage broker for your team.

• Is the major part of your business refinancing? (Anyone can do refinance. This is not what you are looking for.)

• How long have you been a mortgage broker? (You want at least three years experience. It takes experience to know a lot of different lenders and products, and the mortgage industry is constantly changing.)

• Do you work with investors?

• Do you lend on appraised value or purchase price? (Will they lend on the after-repair value?)

• Can you put together 100% financing packages?

• Do you have access to hard money?

• Do you specialize in the nonconforming arena?

• Are you a correspondent lender? (A correspondent lender can lend money for 90 days until lenders complete their funding. They help ensure you won't lose a deal because of last minute problems with the lender's underwriting team. Correspondent lenders get the job done by lending the money themselves.)

• Do you have the ability to fund your own loans? (If they are not familiar with the term "correspondent lender.")

• Would you help me put the deals together? (The mortgage broker can put the deal together for you.)

• Do you have names on file of people who wanted to purchase a home, were qualified in terms of a downpayment but fell short due to their credit scores? How about people who had good credit but could not qualify because of employment history or down payment amounts? Would you be willing to refer those people to me for possible lease option deals and then I would send them back to you when they have improved their scores (or whatever else caused them to be ineligible) for funding at that time?

COMMUNITY BANKER

Your contact at the bank should be someone at the vice president level or another executive with lending authority. Take time to interview several bankers until you find someone you would like to work with.

There are several benefits to using a community bank. First, they have local knowledge of the area and know the growth pattern of the community first-hand. Second, they have local decision-making ability (decisions are not being made in some other state where the person doesn't know your real estate market's potential or the trends of your market). Third, they offer flexibility and are able to be more creative than the larger banks. And fourth, they want to build relationships. Finally, and far from the least important point, they often make what are referred to as LTV loans—loans based upon the value of the property, rather than the amount of the contract and appraisal combined. What does this mean? If you are buying at 70% of FMV, and the appraisal on the house is $100,000, an LTV lender will lend the full amount (and sometimes even more). A conventional lender through your mortgage broker will typically lend a maximum of 80% of the contract price or 80% of the appraisal, whichever gives them the most secure position! Community banks are known for providing great service and will usually tell you why you were turned down if a loan is rejected and work with you to help you overcome that hurdle. They want you to stay with them long time.

Realize that building a solid relationship with the right banker takes time, but the effort is worth it.

CONTRACTOR HANDYMAN

A contractor or handyman can perform the necessary repairs on your properties (investors generally prefer working with a handyman). It is critical that the person or persons you use are licensed and insured to protect you and them. You need to find someone you can trust, and someone who can give you bids and manage the subcontractors.

You can find contacts for the services you need through your local home improvement store's bulletin board or get referral from other investors or individuals you know who have had experience working with contractors or handymen. Another good way to find handymen is through internet sites, including internet referral sites.

TAX PROFESSIONAL

An accountant or CPA can help you take advantage of any available deductions from the ownership of real estate and can help you stay on top of your taxes as a self-employed individual. You need to find one who understands what you are doing and what you are planning to do. And they should be knowledgeable about real estate and tax law, as well as the impact of income taxes and capital gains on what you plan to do. They should also understand corporations and what will help you achieve your financial goals.

APPRAISER

Appraisers are hired to determine the market value of homes when necessary and can help with "Rent to Own" and "Sweat Equity" programs. You want to find an appraiser who will do "subject to" repairs, and who is FHA approved. Appraisers know what needs to be done to qualify for FHA and they know how to bring a property to code. You can learn a great deal from your appraiser.

LAWYER

Your lawyer must be in full-time real estate, mortgage, and corporate law. You want someone who is able to review documents and contracts, and is familiar with rent review and tenant's protection legislation. You also want an attorney who is aggressive in asset protection. You don't want to amass a fortune and then lose it because of a lawsuit. An attorney can also be a great resource for finding deals.

TITLE COMPANY

If you invest in a state where title companies are used, you'll find that a title company can provide you with many beneficial services. For example, they can provide property reports on properties you are thinking of buying. And they can give you information about owners of homes in an area you are "farming." Title companies can also handle closings and provide title insurance to protect you. Sometimes, they are able to pull up pre-foreclosure lists for you. Another advantage of working with a title company is they usually know plenty of investors. Ask them to alert you when deals don't go through.

HOME INSPECTION PROFESSIONAL

Develop a relationship with a home inspection professional. Be sure to accompany the inspector as he or she inspects the house and ask lot of questions. Use a property manager or a real estate professional to help you find a good one.

SURVEYOR

These professionals will survey the land.

A land survey is sometimes necessary to close on the backend.

TERMITE INSPECTORS

Termite inspectors are sometimes necessary for closing and they can alert you to expensive hidden problems. Use a large established company. If the property is treated or was treated within the last year, make sure there is a contract and that it is renewable.

INSURANCE AGENT

An insurance agent can be a great resource in helping you decide the best coverage for your various properties and may be able to direct you to potential deals. Look for an insurance agent who specializes in working with investors.

PROPERT Y MANAGER

If you are buying income properties and don't want to manage them, property managers will be vital to your business. You can learn a lot from property managers, such as the vacancy rate for the area and what the going rent is. Sometimes they will alert you, when an investor they are managing properties for is thinking of selling. They may also be able to give you referral for a good handyman.

GOVERNMENT GRANT AND LOAN SPECIALIST

A government grant and loan specialist can assist you in finding grants and loans that will help you in your real estate investing. You can find them by contacting government agencies or by calling several banks in your area. You may also want to talk to other investors to see what they know and to get referrals.

MENTOR

Model yourself after people who impress you. You will learn much from someone "who has been there" before you. Follow the approach of people who have proven themselves in this business. A mentor could also be a potential investor for you.

NETWORKING
CONTACTS

Network with everyone you know and meet. Hand out business cards whenever possible because leads can come from some of the most unlikely places (for example, stick them inside the envelopes when you pay your bills or leave them with your tip for a waitress). Attend industry-related events such as foreclosure auctions to meet and get to know other investors and communicate regularly with the members of your power team.

And definitely do not miss-out on attending meetings of your local real estate investment club if you have one (if you don't, then consider creating one!). Most real estate investment clubs have a guest speaker and meet once a month. If you have trouble finding a creative lender or another member of your power team, you may get a great referral from a club member. And you can usually find hard money lenders at the meetings.

Check with other investors, title companies, real estate professionals, mortgage brokers, or anyone who is in the real estate business about an investment club in your area. They may charge a monthly or yearly fee for membership. Ask if you can go free on a complimentary visit the first time you attend.

ASSIGNMENT

The following is a suggested assignment. Begin building your power team. Start by building relationships with a real estate professional, a mortgage broker, and a banker. They are critical to your success in real estate investing.

CHAPTER SIX

FINDING MOTIVATED SELLERS

By now you should know how to figure out the true value of a property by using the comps you can get from a real estate professional. You should have started building your power team and are now eager to find a deal. You are ready to make money!

We talked about how you make your money when you buy and the importance of buying right. Buying right would mean getting a great deal to maximize your profit on the backend.

Ultimately, you are going to find what creates a great deal is finding a motivated or flexible seller. In fact, locating motivated sellers and helping them with their problems is the secret to great deals.

WHAT IS A MOTIVATED SELLER?

Motivated sellers are real estate owners who have to sell for one reason or another. There are many factors that affect their motivation to sell and these factors fall into three main categories: personal hardship, the property itself, or economic problems.

What kind of personal hardships may cause a homeowner to become a motivated seller? For one, a owner's failing health may cause him to need to sell the house. Or perhaps the owner has a job out of state and the house is vacant; as time passes, that owner will likely become more flexible on price or terms. Maybe the seller has suffered a job loss and the house is going into foreclosure. Or maybe divorce is forcing a sale. Perhaps the owner died and the house needs to be sold to settle the estate and pay the heirs. Or a partnership has fallen through, causing the need to sell.

The property's condition may create a need to sell as well. Perhaps the owner doesn't have enough money to fix it up. Sometimes a property may have financing that has a balloon payment due and the owner can't refinance it because the property isn't in sufficient condition to qualify for a loan. Or you may find a tired landlord with a house that was trashed by the tenants.

Economic problems can create a need to sell as well. But remember, some economic problems you may encounter can be caused by a change in the economy overall, not just in the economics of the homeowner. For example, a business that employs most of the town, but then goes out of business, will have an impact on real estate in the area. Be careful! You may find phenomenal deals, but are they really great deals if you can't sell the properties or rent them out?

HOW DO WE FIND THEM?

Regardless of the factors that create the need to sell, the point is there are many motivated sellers out there and many ways to find them. In doing so, you can locate a great deal. This chapter offers some techniques you will find helpful in locating flexible sellers in your area.

Work with Real estate professionals

We talked about the importance of having a good real estate agent as a member of your power team and that it may take some time to find the right one. In fact, you may have to try several of them out first before you find the right agent or agents for you, but that's okay. Once you find just a couple of agents who have the ability to locate deals and who will work hard for you, your phone and fax will begin ringing.

Working with real estate agents is usually the best way to locate good deals and motivated sellers when you first start out with real estate investing. Look for the one who knows how to be creative and who specialize in working with investors.

Working with more than one agent

Most investors have more than one agent they work with

because it can be very beneficial to have different agents on your power team. A listing agent, for example, can hold off putting the property on the MLS for a couple of days so an investor has less competition for his or her offer. When you work with an agent who has pocket listings, they may give you first shot at making an offer on a property before they put it on the MLS.

Another type of real estate professional you may find good to work with is a foreclosure specialist. There are banks that work specifically with certain agents in listing their foreclosures. Even though not every foreclosure is a deal, some are worth checking out.

Another real estate professional you may want to work with would be a "hoop jumper" – an agent who is aggressive and works hard for you as a buyer. They will put keywords into the MLS and pull up comps for you.

No matter how many agents you work with, you need to keep one thing in mind: be loyal. If you receive information from one agent and then buy through another agent, you cannot expect that first agent to keep looking for properties for you. Real estate agents have to eat, too. Always buy from the one who gives you the information first. Be loyal to that agent and always create a win/win situation for both of you.

Additionally, some investors try to go around the agent to avoid paying their fees. But this doesn't make good business or moral sense. You need to treat the agent who generates good

leads right by rewarding them and not trying to take away their commission.

Since you will be working with more than one agent, you need to understand that it may be a concern to an agent that he or she will bring you a property, only to have you go directly to the owner or work with another agent. To alleviate this concern, you could offer to sign a Buyer's Broker Agreement. In the agreement, you state you will work with only this agent on the particular property he brought to you for a specific period of time. This protects the agent and keeps him working hard to locate deals for you.

Using keywords

As we've mentioned previously, the real estate professional can put keywords into the remark section of the MLS to find some interesting properties that meet your requirements. For example, the agent can put in the word "motivated" and the computer will give a listing of every property that has the word "motivated" in it.

Keywords you will want the agent to search for include:

• Handyman Special

• Investor Special

• Needs Work

• Offer

• Must Sell

• Needs TLC

• As-Is Condition

• Fixer-Upper

• Motivated

• Divorce

• Illness

• Transferred

• Foreclosure

• Condemned

• Bank Owned

- Desperate

- Estate Sale

- Moving

- Seller Will Finance

- Will Sacrifice

Expired or "aged" listings

Once you have a good relationship with a agent, you can ask him or her to pull up the expired listings or the listings that have been on the market for a while. Sometimes the MLS system will allow your agent to find properties that are free and clear.

Create a flyer to attract aggressive agents

If you want to attract agents who may already have motivated sellers or who know of interesting properties, you may want to run an ad or send a flyer to all the real estate offices in your area of interest.

A sample of what your flyer might look like can be found on the next page.

HOW TO INCREASE YOUR SALES!

Attention: Broker and Real Estate Office Manager!

If you want to MAKE MORE MONEY, then make a copy of this

EXCITING OPPORTUNITY for each of your agents or please post on your board.

WE NEED TO BUY HOUSES AND MULTI-FAMILY UNITS NOW!

We`ll Pay up to 60% of the value with CASH, or more with terms! Any area or condition.

$500 BONUS!

Call us with your properties to sell or sell our properties to your customers and get a $500 BONUS on top of your commissions!

WE HAVE THE EXPERIENCE TO BE SUCCESSFUL.

WE`RE FLEXIBLE, CREATIVE, AND GOOD AT SOLVING PROBLEMS...

We have a WIN/WIN Philosophy! Call me today

Joe Smith, 555-1212

FSBO (For Sale By Owner) Signs By now, you are probably already taking a different route to work every day. You should be paying attention to any FSBO signs you see, especially because some of these properties may not even be listed in the newspaper and the only way to know about them is from the signs. Poorly advertised FSBO homes are an excellent source of leads (think less competition for your offer!). Write down the phone number and call the owner. Better yet, get out of the car and knock on the door.

TRACKING VACANT OR BOARDED HOUSES

Whenever you are in the car, you should be looking for vacant houses, distressed properties, FSBOs, and houses for rent. Drive up and down your target area regularly and seek out these types of properties. Owners of vacant or distressed properties can be motivated sellers.

Write down or tape record the addresses of any vacant or distressed homes you find. You can look up the owner's name at the courthouse. If you have time, stop the car, get out, and knock on neighbors' doors. They may know where the owner has moved to or they may have the owner's phone number. Most neighbors realize this vacant house is bringing down the value of their home and will be anxious to help you locate the owner. If they seem to know how to reach the owner, but are hesitant to give you this information, just give them your business card and ask them to let the owner know you may be interested in purchasing the property.

Leave several flyers at the vacant house. The owner or a family member often checks on the house.

How to find the owners of vacant houses

• Look up the owner's name in tax rolls, appraisal districts, or computerized services. Or check online at: netronline.com. Click on public records, then your county and state. Look for the assessor or auditor's office. Many times, this information is on the Internet.

• Check with the neighbors on both sides of the house and see if they know how to reach the owners or where they have moved.

• Send two letters, one to the address of the vacant house asking it to be forwarded, and the other one to the address with the words "Address Service Requested – Do Not Forward" on the envelope.

• Check with the utility company to see if a new account is open in the previous owner's name.

• Check the phone book or call Information to see if a new phone number has been issued to the owner or if they have a new address.

If you have a different mailing address for the owner, but it isn't listed in the phone book, check a reverse directory, which can be found in the reference section of your public library. The directory starts with addresses first, allowing you to search for the owner's name when the only information you have is their address. Or go to reverseaddress. com. Sometimes the owner may be living with relatives with a different last name and reverse directories can help you find them.

• Employ a private investigator (look in the phone book under Private Investigator) to have them do a skip trace to find the owner. Try to negotiate with them that they must find the information you are looking for or there is no fee.

Auctions

Look in the Yellow Pages and in newspaper advertisements for auctioneers. Call every auctioneer you find and ask them if they auction real estate. If they say yes, ask to be put on their mailing list. If you see an auction for real estate property being advertised or if you receive a notice in the mail from an auctioneer, call and get the address of the property. Drive by the house. If you like the house, make an offer for them to submit before the auction takes place (if the property is bank owned, the bank will wait for the auction to make the sale).

Absolute auctions

There are ABSOLUTE auctions. An absolute auction means they will take whatever is bid. Banks typically have 14 months to sell an REO (Real Estate Owned); if it is not sold by then, they have to quickly unload the property. You usually have to enroll to be able to bid. Get signed up and get a bidder's card.

Foreclosure auctions

Go to a foreclosure auction. If you plan to buy at this auction, be sure to do your due diligence first. You will also probably need cash. There will be lots of competition. This is also a good place to find investors to network with. Go there to meet other investors you can buy from or quick-turn properties to. HUD, VA, FDIC, IRS, and others in some areas of the country, HUD (Department of Housing and Urban Development) and VA (Department of Veteran's Affairs) foreclosure properties are phenomenal deals. In other areas, people pay too much and they are not a deal. To find foreclosure properties offered by HUD, VA, and others, such as the FDIC, the IRS, and Customs, visit the HUD website at www.hud.gov/homes/ homesforsale.cfm. HUD and VA foreclosure bids have to be submitted through a HUDcertified agent/broker.

Important Note: Never bid on an owner occupied list unless you plan to live in the property. If you are not going to live in the property, you need to wait until it appears on the list that is open to all bidders.

Garage Sales

When you see a garage or a yard sale, get out of your car and talk to the owners. Remember what most people do before they put their house up for sale? They de-junk! Someone having a garage sale may be getting ready to sell his or her home. But even if they are not planning on selling, they may know of someone else who is. You will usually find them to be friendly and talkative. Talk to them about the neighborhood. Do they know what houses sell for? Do they know of anyone thinking of selling? Give them your business card.

Court house Records

The courthouse is an excellent source for researching and finding motivated sellers. Get to know where the records are kept in your county courthouse. Sometimes you may be going into different areas of the courthouse depending on what you are researching. Look for: Foreclosures

A foreclosure will inevitably create motivation. As mentioned before, foreclosure doesn't always mean a good deal, but some foreclosure properties are great deals! When working a foreclosure, there are four timeframes that provide profitable opportunities. They will be discussed in greater detail in the chapter on foreclosures.

Private note holders

Many private note holders are investors. They may own several properties or they may be hard moneylenders. Obviously, not all private note holders are investors. But if you see a private note holder with several notes, then you've probably found an investor. A private note holder can become a very motivated seller if they have to foreclose on a property they hold.

Divorce cases

Divorce is a primary cause of foreclosure. Even if a couple does not lose their house to foreclosure, divorce can cause great financial You must have full disclosure with both sellers jointly signing any agreement.

Out-of-state owners

If you can find an out-of-state owner, you may find a more flexible seller. It can be a hassle to manage a property from a distance. Or sometimes the owner had to move quickly and now the house is sitting vacant. Sometimes a title company will have the ability to pull this information up for you from the county records.

Houses with tax liens

When an owner is having trouble paying their taxes, it is usually a sign they are having financial difficulty. Often, there is a lot of equity in the home and you could help solve their problem and make it a win/win situation.

Lis Pendens

Lis Pendens is Latin for "suit pending," referring to a court action. In some states, it is the beginning stage of foreclosure.

Probate sales and estate sales

With probate and estate sales, property can be purchased from the estate of an individual who has passed away. Sometimes good deals can be found in circumstances where there is no will or known heirs and the state is liquidating the estate's assets. However, if there is a will, there can also be great deals if the heirs and beneficiaries are just looking to liquidate assets so they can disperse an inheritance. This can be a huge opportunity for an investor, especially when heirs live out of town. The heirs may not want the property or they may not be able to afford it. Many times, the family tells the executor of the estate to just get rid of the property and the heirs are often willing to take a large discount on it. And sometimes the executor has to sell the property to pay off debts and taxes. Contact the executor of the will. You can find contact information in the county recorder's office or in public notices in the legal section of your newspaper.

Bankruptcies

You can find information about bankruptcies in legal papers or at the bankruptcy court. The name of the trustee who has been appointed to handle the case will appear in the papers and the notice should tell if real estate is involved. The trustee will give you the information if you call. Creditors will usually take huge discounts. Even if the bankruptcy has been recently filed and is not closed, the court can release the property.

Eviction filings

Go to your county courthouse and ask the clerk where to find the department to file an eviction complaint. A landlord can become a motivated seller after going through an eviction and may welcome an offer from an investor who is providing a way out of ever having to go through one again.

Local Newspapers

You should be checking the classified section of your local newspaper on a daily or almost daily basis. Nationwide, the classified ads are filled with real estate properties for sale. A small percentage of these ads are placed by owners who are slightly motivated to sell. An even smaller percentage only 1 to 2%) of the ads are placed by sellers who are desperate and intensely motivated. These are the sellers you want to talk to.

In the beginning, you may think there are no motivated sellers in your area, but be persistent and keep calling. Most investors check a few ads and then give up. Don't let that be you! Make the effort and reap the benefits.

You should also "grade" the ads, looking for motivated sellers by using the keywords mentioned throughout this manual. Start by circling or highlighting any word that might indicate a motivated seller, a distressed property, or special financing terms, such as "must sell," "will look at all offers," "investor special," "needs TLC," "rent to own," "owner finance," "no qualifying," or "take over payments." The ads with your target keywords can be your "A" list, your top picks to call first. Call all the FSBO ads that depict the keywords showing that either the property or the owner is distressed or that there may be creative financing available.

You'll soon find that your search for good leads is much more effective when you know exactly what you are looking for.

Place a "goldmine" ad

In addition to being a source of finding houses for sale, newspapers can be a way of generating deals when savvy investors place their own ads in the paper. Getting the seller to call you is extremely important. This can save you time and give you a good deal. An example of a goldmine ad follows:

Private investor looking to buy income properties.

Will look at all, any condition.

CAN PAY CASH
555-1212

As a buyer, you want to get the seller to call you! You can place these ads in the Real Estate Wanted section or in the Houses For Sale section of your local newspaper and real estate magazines. Additionally, if your town has a "Thrifty Nickel," "Penny Saver," "Shopper's Guide," or similar paper, these could be great places for your ad in the same sections listed above. When people are desperate to sell, they will often look in the small newspapers. (We have also provided other sample ads for you throughout this manual.)

Use legal newspapers

Legal newspapers are another way to find motivated sellers, as people who are struggling with bankruptcy, foreclosure, divorce, etc. will be in the legal notices. See if your local library has a copy or ask how you can find the legal newspaper by talking to title companies, attorneys, and banks.

When you find the legal notices, you may want to contact these potentially motivated sellers with a simple letter. Your letter might read like the following:

I understand you have recently gone through some difficult circumstances in your life and may be interested in selling your home. If you are interested, please call me at 555-1212.

People who are having difficulties will often look in the legal publication to see if their notice is in the paper, so consider running an ad in a legal publication. You may find attorneys will also start calling, asking for a business card to pass on to their clients.

I Buy Houses Any Area, Any Condition

CASH

Completely Confidential Call 555-1212

"Bird Dogs"

Bird dogs are referrals who act as your eyes and ears looking for leads on your behalf. You might also hear this referred to as "ant farming." For the hard work they provide, you pay them a finder's fee.

Who can be your potential bird dogs? Think of the people who are out in the neighborhoods every day, such as the mail carrier and the cable installer. These people are regularly going into your prime target areas. You may also consider talking to garbage collectors, meter readers, lawn service workers, pizza deliverers, newspaper deliverers, code enforcement officers, firefighters, and more.

Create flyers and reward cards

To help you find potential bird dogs, create simple flyers and reward cards to attract them to the opportunity and explain the benefits of your bird dog program.

To get the flyers noticed, you may want to use fluorescent colored paper. For the reward cards, it may be best to use doublesided business cards to make them easy to pass out. If your doublesided business cards can have a fluorescent colored front and a white back, it will help them stand out from the average business card.

Here's an example of how your reward card might read:

$CASH REWARD$

$250.00

Bring me any vacant or boarded houses.

Everywhere you go, hand your reward card out. When you go out to dinner, put one with the tip. When you see the mail carrier, stop and give him or her a card.

Additionally, hand out a flyer listing the fees you would pay your bird dog. A sample flyer might include the following information:

• Make $5 every time you bring us the address of a vacant or boarded up house whether we buy it or not.

• Make $10 every time you bring us a Polaroid picture with the address of a vacant or boarded up house whether we buy it or not.

• Make $250 every time you bring us the address of a vacant or boarded up house and we buy it (paid at closing only). Exceptions: Please be advised that we do not accept properties in the following areas:

BIRD DOG FEES SAMPLE FLYER

CASH REWARD

$250.00

Bring me any vacant or boarded houses.

Fluorescent color front with black lettering.

I WILL PAY
$250.00
every time I
buy one!

Don't bring me any agent signs.
Call
555-1212

White background and black lettering.

_____ *or those with an agent sign on them or those addresses already submitted by other bird dogs. All bird dogs are paid upon a first-come, first-served basis.*

NICHE MARKETING

Signs

A fluorescent yellow sign with black writing attracts attention. Make it a simple one-line ad that can easily be read from a distance and include your phone number. Post your signs wherever you are allowed in your city. For example, post signs on or at:

• Bus stop benches

• Community billboards (use small signs)

• Stadium seating

• Movie theaters

• Take out menus

• Grocery store carts

• Utility posts or telephone poles (best when they are posted up high)

• Major intersections (use surveyor stakes to put them in the ground)

You can go to an office supply store and buy a package of fluorescent paper (8-1/2 x 11 sheets – 100 sheet packages) for your signs. Place them in plastic sheet protectors and staple them on telephone poles. Or use plastic corrugated sheets (lightweight, but sturdy sheets of plastic) for your signs and attach them with roofing nails. Make sure you are not violating any city codes.

Example signs might be:

I BUY HOUSES FOR CASH
555-1212

In the beginning, you will need to have an answering machine. The message they get when they call might be something like:

"Hi! I'm Jimmy. If you're interested in buying or selling a house…"

Later, you may want to use an answering service; people like to talk to a live person.

Flyers

Design an 8-½ x 11-inch flyer and distribute it door to door in the neighborhoods where you want to buy. The flyer should read like an ad:

"We buy houses, fast cash, fast closing times, any condition, any price, 555-1212."

You can hire students or people from your local labor board to distribute the flyers. Two people can put out 500 flyers in three hours. Put your flyers on every door in the neighborhood. Car windows and mailboxes are off limits.

Door hangers

People generally respond well to door hangers. Most printers will design and cut them out for you. Hire someone to deliver them or incorporate passing them out into an exercise routine and do it yourself.

Bulletin boards

Put flyers anywhere you see bulletin boards, such as grocery stores, laundromats, restaurants, the community center, the unemployment office, a city center, and mail centers. Every time you enter a business place, look to see if they offer a community bulletin board where you can post your information.

Car washes

Ask the manager if they can hand out your flyers. Offer to pay them per car.

Handouts

You can provide handouts wherever you are, wherever it is allowed. You may be able to distribute handouts at some school or local events, for example.

Magnetic car signs

Put magnetic car signs on your car. It can give you credibility to be in the neighborhood.

We buy houses cash or terms phone

Check with your car insurance company to see if you need to change your coverage (some car insurance companies will consider it a vehicle used for business if you display a magnetic car sign and you will need to have that in the policy).

Drive for dollars

As you are driving around looking for vacant houses, have your signs in the back of your car along with a staple gun and tape. Every time you see a vacant house, not only should you be writing down the address, but you should also get out of the car and put a sign on the vacant house (the wording can be the same as the magnetic car sign). Make sure the signs are large enough to be read from the street. We are not only trying to get the vacant homeowner to call; we also want motivated sellers who happen to see our sign to call us.

Cooperative advertising

Have you ever received mail that contains advertisements for several companies in one envelope, like Valpak? Everyone shares in the production costs, reducing your own cost. Make sure the message is simple. The mailing company may have people on staff who can help you design your ad.

Align yourself with a couple of banks or credit unions. Talk to the branch manager and tell them you are involved in mailings and ask them to join you. Tell them that every week, you will go to the Chamber of Commerce and pull out leads and send their information along with yours. Suggest that their part of the deal be to pay for the postage.

Direct mail

Make sure that when you mail to people in your target area, you do repeat mailings. It usually takes four mailings for most people to respond. If you want to target a specific area, you can get a list of owners and addresses from your title company. Some people will use a reverse address book.

Yellow page listings

Successful investors advertise in the same section as real estate professionals. Make

sure, you advertise that if they call you, they will not be paying a commission. You want to stand out from the crowd.

Listing publications

Consider placing a small display ad approximately 1" x 2" in your Sunday newspaper's free TV listings guide. The cost is usually quite reasonable.

Radio and television

Most cable programming offers a TV listings channel showing what will be on for that day. The top of the screen is usually devoted to continuous advertising or advertising mixed with a few TV news-related programs. In some markets, the cost of advertising on this channel can be relatively inexpensive, especially during non-peak times. This is often the best time to advertise, when people who can't sleep turn on the TV.

Additionally, you may want to considerradio advertising, which is another great way to market your business, usually with less competition for your services.

Restrooms

In some public restrooms, low-cost advertising is offered on the back of the stall doors.

Business cards

Your business cards should say something simple and to the point like:

I BUY HOUSES, CASH, ANY CONDITION

or

I BUY AND SELL HOUSES

or

WE BUY HOUSES CASH!

Or

WE SOLVE REAL ESTATE PROBLEMS

You want your business cards to clearly state what you do. Avoid phrases like "real estate investor" which means nothing to a motivated seller. They are only interested in what you can do for them: I BUY HOUSES, CASH! Your name should be the smallest information on the card. Hand them out everywhere, such as restaurants, barbershops or salons, stores, and offices. You should be ordering new cards every three months or you are not getting the best use out of them.

NETWORKING RESOURCES

Banks, mortgage companies, credit and finance The people at these businesses deal regularly with investors and, quite often, are investors themselves. They sometimes have REOs (real estate owned – bank owned properties), foreclosures, and other leads.

Private lenders

Private lenders can be more than a great financial resource; they can also be a resource for potential deals. As more and more buyers turn to them instead of banks and traditional mortgage companies for loans, many of these private lenders start to build an inventory of foreclosed properties when those loans default. Sometimes they just want to cash out.

Title companies

Title companies close for other investors. By networking with them, you can often find out what other investors are doing. Ask the title company to let you know when deals don't go through and to alert you to those opportunities.

Relocation directors

When an employee of a large corporation is relocated, the

company will often market or buy the employee's previous home as part of their relocation package. These corporations become extremely motivated to unload these homes. To find them, start by mailing letters to the relocation directors of major employers in your area. You will need to get the address for the corporate headquarters, which may be out of state. Let them know what you are looking for. If they don't have anything at this time, ask them to keep your letter on file so they can contact you if something in your area becomes available.

Propert y managers

Property managers often manage properties for out-of-state investors who may be tired of owning property in another state or for investors who don't take care of their properties for any number of reasons. Many property managers also actively invest in property themselves. Network with these individuals; they always come across deals and are a great resource if you end up needing property management yourself. Remember, as managers of properties for other investors, they are in a good position to let you know of investors who are looking to sell and to tell you what's right or wrong with their properties.

City code enforcement

Get a list of houses with code violations from them. They tag the houses, so they know before everyone else which ones are vacant or have a code violation. In some regions, the city council has a website and you can pull up the minutes from their council meetings. The code enforcement person has to fill out a daily form.

Appraisers

You can learn a lot from appraisers, such as what needs to be done to qualify for FHA. An appraiser also knows when deals won't work because the house doesn't meet code. They know a lot of investors and sometimes hear of deals.

Attorneys

Contact bankruptcy attorneys. The attorney doesn't care what the property sells for; they get the same amount of money regardless. And most of them only have two or three investors they know to contact with opportunities. In bankruptcy cases, the owner usually wants or needs the property sold quickly. Usually they will settle for pennies on the dollar.

Contact attorneys who handle probate (check the Yellow Pages). Get on their contact list to be the first person they call to sell the property. They want CASH – the advantage you want to give them is that you can buy with cash.

Additionally, attorneys know of people who are having financial or legal problems and need to sell their real estate. Contact attorneys who specialize in real estate, foreclosure, estate planning, and divorce. Network with them and ask them to refer your services!

Accountants

Accountants work with people having financial or tax problems. They will most likely not give out names, but they may be willing to give your name to their clients.

Insurance agents

Insurance agents have clients facing issues such as fire and water damage, vacant homes, and mold. These situations can create motivation on the part of the owner of such a house, and some-times the insurance company and lender. If they know you buy these kinds of properties, they may be more than happy to pass this information on to their clients.

Bail bondsmen

When bail bondsmen bail people out of jail, some of those people will have money and some of them will have property. Send postcards to the bondsmen in your area. If they own a lot of properties, they put signs out to get more people calling. They are used to buying and selling and they get properties really cheap. They usually buy for collateral and sell when they have too much inventory.

Health and senior services

Health and senior services workers often take care of people who have no family to leave their properties to. In some cases, the nursing homes have the right to sell the assets. This is one time when you definitely cannot put "and/or assigns." The judge wants to know who bought the property. Contact the manager or the executors. Send a postcard:

Attn: Nursing Home Director We buy homes CASH

Charitable organizations – a hidden market!

When a person donates real estate to a church or charitable organization, the appraised value is tax deductible. There is a four-year hold for the full tax deduction. If a church or charitable organization sells at a discounted price before the four-year period, the person who donates will not get the full deduction, so churches and charitable organizations are left holding a lot of property, but they need the cash. They can't sell at a discount until after the four-year period or no one would donate. You might send a letter that reads:

To whom it may concern:

Hello, My name is _____. I am a local real estate investor in your area. I am writing you to inquire about charitable donated properties you may have in the church's portfolio. If your church has any single family homes or investment properties that have been donated, I may be interested in making an offer on any or all of them.

Thank you for your consideration in this matter.

Sincerely,

Condemned and fire damaged properties

Contact the health department, fire marshal, and the city code enforcement department to locate these types of properties.

Investors and investment clubs

Investors are a great source for both buyers and sellers. For example, wholesalers (see the chapter on wholesaling) are always looking to quick-turn property and can lead you to some great deals.

Too many investors don't want to work with other investors. This is ridiculous. Somehow they have false notion they will be supporting their competition if they share ideas or make deals with each other, but that just makes them miss out on some amazing win/ win opportunities. In fact, the most successful wholesale investors work almost exclusively with other investors. They recognize that they don't have to spend all their time working with potential homeowners who are often unsophisticated when it comes to real estate; they can instead work with investors who understand the business, who can move quickly on deals, and who know how to spot good deals when they see them.

The bottom line is networking with other investors can be both educational and profitable.

To begin building relationships with other investors, look for their ads in local newspapers and contact real estate investment clubs in your local area. Ask investors, bankers, and real estate agents if they know where a local investment club meets. Attending club meetings is a great way to sharpen your real estate skills, network with like-minded individuals, and find great deals.

Clubs usually meet once a month and have a guest speaker who may provide valuable information about your area. But don't judge the club by the speaker; look at the investors attending. Who are the members? How can they help you? Are they friendly?

Most clubs charge a monthly or yearly fee to members, so ask if you can go free on a complimentary first visit. At investor clubs, you will be able to find referrals to build your power team. You may find deals, a hard moneylender, or creative financing. Locating a good one is worth the effort.

Now go out and find a motivated seller and get a great deal!

REVIEW

The secret to great deals is finding a motivated seller. We do not want to waste time working with sellers who are not flexible with their price or terms.

We find these sellers in many ways:

• Use a Realtor

– Work with more than one agent

– Have the real estate professional search the MLS using the keywords you have learned

– Create a flyer to attract aggressive agents

• FSBO Signs

– Take different routes while driving in the car

– Write down the phone number and call or knock on the door

• Tracking Vacant or Boarded Houses

– Drive up and down your target area

– Write down addresses of any vacant or distressed properties

– Locate the owner

– Talk to neighbors

– Check county records

– Send out letters

– Check with the utility company

– Check the phone book or call in formation

– Check a reverse directory if you have a mailing address and want a phone number

– Look on the Internet

– Do a skip trace

• Auctions

– Call auctioneers and ask to be put on their mailing list

– Can make an offer before the auction

– Check out absolute auctions

• Foreclosure Auctions

– Attend an auction

– Research the property with due diligence if you plan on buying

– Good place to meet and network with other investors

• HUD, VA, FDIC, IRS

– Visit the HUD website: www.hud. gov/homes/homesforsale.

– Bids must be submitted by an approved real estate professional

– Good deals in some areas of the country

– Do not bid on owner occupied list unless you intend to live in the house

• Garage Sales

– People get rid of their junk before they sell

– Get out and talk with the owners

– Ask about the neighborhood and may be thinking of selling

• Court house

- Foreclosures

- Private note holders

- Owners of vacant houses

- Divorce

- Out-of-state owners

- Houses with tax liens

- Lis Pendens

- Probate sales

- Estate sales

- Bankruptcies

- Eviction filings

• Local Newspaper

- Check out the classifieds

- Place a goldmine ad

- Legal newspaper

• Bird Dogs

- Let others be your "eyes and ears"

- Pass out flyers

- Mail carrier

- Cable installer

- Garbage collector

- Meter reader

- Lawn services

- Pizza delivery

- Paper carrier
- Code enforcement
- Firefighter
- Offer a finder's fee
• Niche Marketing
- Signs
- Flyers
- Door hangers
- Bulletin boards
- Car washes
- Handouts
- Magnetic car signs
- Drive for dollars
- Cooperative advertising
- Direct mail
- Yellow Pages
- TV listing publications
- Radio and television ads
- Restrooms
- Business cards
• Networking
- Banks, mortgage companies, credit, and finance
- Private lenders
- Title companies

- Relocation director s
- Property managers
- Section 8
- City code enforcement
- Appraisers
- Attorneys
- Accountants
- Insurance agents
- Bail bondsmen
- Health and senior services
- Charitable organizations
- People who serve legal documents
- Condemned and fire damaged properties
- Investors and investment clubs

CHAPTER SEVEN

MAKING QUICK CASH: WHOLESALES

Wholesaling is immediate money in your pocket. When you wholesale a property, you are buying and selling, not buying, fixing, and selling. You do not need to get a loan to buy the property. You never fix it up. You don't have to put a lot of time and work into the house. You simply put the property under contract and sell it to a buyer without ever having purchased it. Once you have a property under contract, you should be able to have a "payday" a week to ten days later! This is called quick-turning a property. When you wholesale, you are using a buy low, sell low strategy. The type of real estate you will be looking at will be considerably below market value. These properties can be single family or multi-family homes, but most of the properties you wholesale will be single family. This is because there is a larger inventory of single family homes to pick from and your buyer, the investor, will most likely be more interested in the single family homes.

You will find your best deals in properties that are vacant, abandoned, or boarded up – properties no one is really looking to buy. Banks won't finance condemned properties. Insurance companies won't insure them. Most real estate agents won't list them. You should be targeting these types of houses. Properties like this usually have motivated sellers. For some reason the owners are unable to take care of them or just don't want them.

The houses don't have to be boarded up, just rundown and unable to be financed. You are targeting problem properties. You want properties that are physically distressed.

Sounds pretty bad – nothing you really want to fix up, so why are we talking about these types of houses? Don't we stress "cosmetic work only?"

Some of the properties may only need cosmetic repair, but many will need major renovations. They may be in marginal neighborhoods. What you need to remember is:

There Is No Fix-Up. We Buy And Sell As-Is!

Remember, the key to any real estate deal is buying right. With wholesaling, you buy them ugly and sell them ugly to investors, maximizing your profits with minimal effort.

Now that's definitely buying right!

WHERE TO FIND WHOLESALE DEALS

In the last chapter, we discussed how to locate motivated sellers and, in doing so, find the "deal." Use the ideas given there to help you locate this kind of property. In the meantime, here is a quick review of the techniques we have found most useful in

finding wholesale deals:

• Read and advertise in your local newspapers

– Check out the classifieds

– Place a goldmine ad

– Use the legal newspaper

– Use bird dogs (pass out flyers and offer a finder's fee)

– Mail carrier

– Cable worker

– Garbage collector

– Meter reader

– Lawn service worker

– Pizza deliverer

– Paper carrier

- Code enforcement officer

- Firefighter

• Market your services whenever, wherever possible

- Signs

- Flyers

- Door hangers

- Bulletin boards

- Car washes

- Handouts

- Magnetic car signs

- Direct mail

- Business cards

• Drive for dollars (see the next section)

DRIVING FOR DOLLARS

Pick the areas of town that are known for having distressed properties (identify two to five neighborhoods that would have these types of properties). You will be looking at low to moderate class neighborhoods and "we care" neighborhoods. These are the areas where you will find investors rehabbing and where you might see Habitat for Humanity building affordable homes. Look for areas that have a lot of renters. Homeowners living there have usually lived there for several years and many have their homes paid for.

Once you have identified the areas with these characteristics, you will be "driving for dollars" (literally driving around, looking for profitable deals). As you drive in your car, look up and down each street trying to locate vacant or abandoned houses. You can easily spot these kinds of properties. Look for:

• Tall grass, leaves all over, snow not plowed

• Lots of newspapers in the yard, at the bottom of the driveway, or on the porch

• No curtains or window coverings

• Broken windows, boarded up windows and doors

• City or county stickers

• Abandoned automobiles, junk in the yard

- Missing utility meters (electric, gas, water)

- Flyers stuck in the door

- Property in bad shape – needs work (might be "ugly")

- Mail piled up in the mailbox

While you are driving for dollars, write down the addresses of the distressed properties you find. And be sure to talk to neighbors, mail carriers, cable workers, and utility workers. Create a "reward flyer" and hand it out. Here's an example of how your reward flyer might read:

CASH REWARD

$250.00

For finding vacant and boarded up houses. Any area. Any condition.

555-1212

Let others be your bird dogs – your eyes and ears. Offer them a reward for helping you achieve success.

Tell everyone in your world what you are doing! Talk to the grocery store clerk, your hairdresser or barber, people at your church, those you work with, and the waitress where you dine. Let all your friends know what you are doing. Get the word out!

Additionally, put magnetic car signs on your vehicle. Many of our students have had tremendous success making money simply off calls from people who saw their magnetic car signs.

While driving for dollars, you should also have signs in the back of your car along with a staple gun and some tape. Make the words bold and large enough so they can be read from the street. Too many words will make it harder to read. Keep the wording simple, such as:

WE BUY HOUSES CASH Phone

Use colorful, fluorescent paper to attract attention. We want everyone to see these signs. If a house is boarded up, staple the sign on one of the boards. If it isn't boarded up, but it is abandoned, tape the sign on a window. If the house has "no trespassing" sign, then don't put the sign up. Try to place the signs where they can be easily seen and read, even from the street. You want people with unwanted houses calling you! You can also have surveyor stakes that you can attach the sign to and place in the ground at intersections in very visible areas. When you drive for dollars, you are not only trying to find distressed properties, but you are also letting everyone know you buy houses.

$ CASH $ FOR HOUSES

Any Area, Any Condition CALL NOW! Phone # When you find a vacant home, ask the neighbors if they know how you can reach the owner (see How to Find the Owners of Vacant Houses in the previous chapter). Or you can go to the courthouse where the property taxes are paid to see if you can find their names. They may have a different mailing address.

ASSIGNMENT OF CONTRACT AND DOUBLE CLOSING

There are two ways you can wholesale a property. You will either do an assignment of contract or a double closing (also referred to as a simultaneous closing).

Assignment of Contract

With an assignment of contract, you will have two contracts. One will be a purchase and sale contract between you and the seller of the property. In this assignable contract, you will put your name plus the additional words "and/or assigns" beside it (i.e, John Smith and/or assigns). This gives you the right to assign the contract. The idea here is you have used your expertise to negotiate a fantastic deal with the seller and now you are assigning your right to make that deal on the terms you have negotiated to someone else, your buyer.

The second contract will be between you and your buyer and is called an assignment of contract. An assignment of contract will have the address of the property, as well as information about the seller, about you as the original buyer, and about the buyer you are assigning the contract to. It will also have the amount your buyer is paying you to assign him or her the contract (the fee you are charging for having found and made this great deal that you are passing along). The typical fee for an assignment of contract is around $3,000 to $5,000. However, students have made $10,000 or more (when your profit is this high, you will want to do a double closing instead, which we will discuss in a moment).

When you assign the contract, you will make sure you collect a non-refundable deposit. If you can collect the full assignment fee at that time, by all means take it. Otherwise, try to get half of the fee or at least $1,000 to $2,000. That way, if for some reason your buyer backs out, you still have made some money.

In essence, what you have done is sold your purchase contract to your buyer. You never own the property, you should not have to pay closing costs, and your name will not appear on the deed. You get the property under contract, assign the contract, and make money. It's a terrific and very popular way to make money in real estate.

Double Closing (or Simultaneous Closing)

Because your buyer will know how much money you are making with an assignment of contract, you will want to make sure you don't care if he or she has this information.

Most investors and sellers will not mind you making some money. You should be paid for your expertise and foresight. But if they think you are making too much money, they may try to go behind your back or not work with you again. So generally speaking, when you are going to be making a lot of money on the deal (say, more than $7,000), you will do what's called a double closing (or simultaneous close).

With a double closing, you will have two purchase and sale contracts. You will have one between you and the seller of the property. The other purchase and sale contract will be between you and your buyer. This is how it works: You actually buy the property and sell it in a simultaneous closing to your buyer. The title company or closing attorney handles the transaction for you, making everything happen simultaneously and smoothly, but without ever having you, your buyer, or the seller together at the same table. Your buyer will usually be asked to come in first to close with you as the seller. They will bring the money that is needed to purchase the property (you will later use this money to pay the seller). The money given to the title company or lawyer sits in a trust until the original seller of the property comes to sign their paperwork associated with you as the buyer. You will come in last and sign both sides of the transaction (as a seller and as a buyer). The seller will only see the transaction between you and him or her. Likewise, your buyer will only see the contract between the two of you. There will be closing costs that you may have to pay.

CONTINGENCIES

Note: This section offers only general guidelines no legal advice is being offered. Always consult with your local attorney for guidance.

Because the properties you are looking at to wholesale are not the sort of properties you really want to buy, you will want to use contingencies ("subject to") to protect yourself if you don't find a buyer (consult a lawyer for assistance).

In both the assignment of contract and the double closing, you will use the same contingencies and conditions in your addendum.

In the addendum, you may consider adding these contingencies and conditions."

• Sale is contingent upon inspection and approval of bids by Buyer and Buyer's partner to be completed in writing within _____ business days.

• Upon acceptance of the offer, buyer to receive key to the property and have the right to show to any and all prospective occupants.

Use this second contingency is generally used if it is a FSBO. If the property is listed with a real estate professional, put:

• Buyer to receive access to the property upon acceptance of the offer.

If the FSBO house is not vacant, then put in a clause of:

• Buyer shall have access to the property for the purpose of showing the property to prospective occupants and to obtain bids on repairs.

An optional contingency you may add (be aware that too many "subject to" clauses can kill a deal):

• It is agreed that Buyer has 30 business days from the date of this offer to perform due diligence. This may include determining any needed repairs, researching the title, and confirming market value. In the event the Buyer determines that the property does not meet with his/her approval, the contract will become null and void, and the Buyer's deposit returned immediately.

When doing an assignment of contract, give yourself as long of a closing date as you can (preferably at least 45 to 60 days). If you don't have a buyer within two to three weeks, back out of the deal. We don't want to hurt people and get the reputation of tying up properties and never purchasing them.

TITLE COMPANIES OR CLOSING ATTORNEYS

A critical element in being able to do an assignment of contract or a double closing is having a good closing officer who knows how to do them. Start calling title companies (or attorneys if your state uses attorneys for real estate closings). You will need to get past the front desk and speak to the actual person who handles the closings. Ask them if they have worked with investors. Can they do assignment of contracts or double closings? Have they ever done them before?

Do not be discouraged if they don't seem to know what you are talking about. It is not uncommon for title companies and even some attorneys to be unfamiliar with double closings and assignment of contracts.

If you feel like giving up, don't; just keep calling until you find one who understands what you want to do. Sometimes it helps to get a referral from an investor who has done this before. Make sure the closing agent understands you do not plan to bring any money to the closing table when you are talking about double closings. You are simply bringing two purchase contracts: one between the seller and you, the other between you and your buyer. Ask them what they would charge you to handle this type of transaction.

Also, ask if they charge you to do an assignment of contract. Routinely, it will be the seller and your buyer who pay the closing costs. You are just the middleman and once you have assigned the contract, you are out of the deal except for the fact that they will cut you a check for the agreed upon fee that is listed in the assignment of contract.

Ask the closing agent if they have had any problems doing an assignment of contract or a double closing. They may tell you that when your buyer's lender looks at the assignment of contract, they may say, "Who is this Joe Buyer? We want the contract between Sally Seller and Jim (your new) Buyer. Get Joe out of the way." Well that will work if Sally Seller is willing to redo the contract. Otherwise you have a problem!

There are many reasons why we want to work with an investor:

• An investor does not have to "fall in love with the property." They will crunch the numbers and if it's a great deal, they want it.

• Investors have access to to hard money or cash. Hard money and cash don't care if it's an assignment of contract or a double closing. You should build a database of hard money lenders for you to use if later on you want to buy, fix, and sell, and for your buyers (if a buyer needs hard money to close the deal, you can refer him or her to the hard money lender).

• You will also like dealing with investors because cash or hard money means a quick closing. Would you not rather have a paycheck a week after finding your buyer instead of waiting 30 days?

BUILDING A
DATABASE OF BUYERS

You may be worrying, "How will I find the buyer?" Finding the buyer is the easy part when you have the right price accepted. When you wholesale, it is not location, location, location. Rather, it is the deal, the deal, the deal! If you can buy it cheap enough, you will have an investor who will want the property. In fact, investors will keep coming back to you for more.

When you wholesale a property, you should create a database of buyers. Don't panic if you find an exceptional deal and you don't have any investors in your database. You should have no problem finding a buyer who will want to purchase the property. If there is money for the investor to make, he or she will want it. However, you should start networking with other investors and building your database as soon as you possibly can.

There are many ways and places for you to find investors for your database, including:

• Investment clubs

• Auctions

• Properties with "For Rent" signs (write down phone numbers and call)

• Talk to people rehabbing a home and ask who the owner is (probably an investor)

• People who call off your signs

• Real estate professionals, title companies, attorneys, appraisers, contractors, bankers

• Calling the "I buy" ads

• Advertising

The following offers a little more insight into how to tap these sources for your database.

Real estate investment clubs

When you attend your local investment club, you need to network with the investors there. These are potential buyers for your deals. You will find endless possibilities when you rub shoulders with other investors.

Tell everyone what you are planning on doing and see who is interested. Ask them what types of properties they are interested in and in what areas. Ask them if you can call them when you find a property you think fits their requirements.

Auctions

Attend a real estate auction. You will see other investors there. Talk to them. Get their business cards and give them yours. Again, your goal is to find out what kind of investing they do to see how you can work with them. Let them know what you do and tell them you come across phenomenal deals but you simply cannot buy everything you find. Tell them you will gladly contact them when you find a property they may be interested in purchasing.

Properties with "For Rent" signs

Properties that are offered for rent are oftened owned by investors. Perhaps they are looking to purchase additional properties. It never hurts to call and ask.

Talk to rehabbers

If you see someone rehabbing a property, ask them if they are an investor. You might find yourself talking to the investor or with a member of his or crew. If an investor is rehabbing a property in one of the areas you are focusing on, then he or she may want a deal you find in that same area or one similar to the property they're already working on. Let the investor know you are just starting out and that you will be looking for houses that need to be rehabbed. Ask them if they would like you to contact them when you find a rehab for a good price. Most would be happy to have you bring them a good deal. You save them time researching so they can spend more time rehabbing.

Real estate professionals, bankers, appraisers, lawyers, etc.

Professional people who are in the real estate business know investors. They are people you want to interact with.

Call the "I Buy" ads

Call all the "I buy" ads you see in the newspaper, such as advertisements that read: "I buy houses. Pay cash. Any area, any condition." There are usually two categories of people who place these ads:

1) wholesalers – buy low and sell low; and

2) retailers – buy, fix, and sell properties or buy, fix, and keep properties.

When you talk to the wholesalers:

• Tell them you're looking to buy some properties

• Let them know you are a new investor in town and you need some deals

• Ask them if they have any inventory (properties for sale)

• If they have inventory, ask them to fax you a list of the

properties they have for sale

Next, drive-by the properties. Now you will see where these wholesalers are finding the good deals and where wholesale deals are being done in a short period of time. You will find that wholesalers typically farm an area. Usually, they concentrate in two to three different areas. You'll also see how much they're asking for the properties and what type of houses they have.

Call them back and say:

"I might be interested in some of the properties you have for sale. I like working with investors. I don't care how much money you are going to make on a deal as long as I get the deal I need. By the way, the properties here on the list, are you going to be assigning them or do you already own them?"

If they say they're an assignment of contract, figure they paid about $3,000 less than what they're asking. If they say they own it (they may not – but they may want more money), figure they paid about $10,000 less than what they're asking. Ask them if they have any funding sources (hard money lenders). Now we're finding a potential funding source for us to borrow money from. We are also finding a funding source for our buyer to use.

When you talk to the retailers:

• Ask them what kind of properties they are looking for

• Find out if they are into major rehab or a little fix-up

• Ask what areas they are focusing on

• Find out what price range they prefer

Whatever you do, don't become a real estate agent for other investors! Don't waste time looking for the "one" property an investor wants. It is helpful to know what they are looking for and where, but find great deals and let everyone know what you have.

Be sure to get their phone numbers, fax, email, etc. so you can reach them quickly.

ADVERTISE TO FIND YOUR BUYER

As we mentioned before, don't panic if you don't have any investors in your database right now. In fact, many investors find a great deal and get an offer accepted without having a potential buyer lined up. They know if the price is right, it will not be difficult to wholesale the property. Again, this goes back to the idea of buying right. If they have figured in a good range of profit for an investor, investors will want the property. In these cases, to find their potential buyer, they simply place an ad in the newspaper. To attract investors, the ad should state what the property is worth fixed up and how much you are asking for it (what you have it under contract for plus your profit). When the investor sees a huge spread and calculates his or her potential for profit in purchasing your property, your phone should start ringing off the hook!

Here are a couple of sample ads:

Dr. Dennis Mulumba

3 bdr 2 bath
Terrace Park Area
Worth $160K

WILL
SACRIFICE
FOR $100K

Call
555-1212

3 bdr 2 bath
Valued At $80K
FIRE SALE
$40K
Cash Buyers Only
555-1212

\

Once you have started working on a database of potential buyers for the properties you want to wholesale, be sure to use a system that is organized and includes their names, phone numbers, fax number, email, and other pertinent information, such as what types of properties they are looking for, what areas they like to invest in, and what price range they prefer. Included in this chapter is a Buyer Tracking Sheet for you to use until you find the system that works best for you.

WHAT TO OFFER

When wholesaling a property, how do you figure out what to offer? Here is a formula you can use:

What is the After-Repair Value (ARV)

$_____

 ubtract repairs –

$_____

Subtract profit for the investor –

$_____

If ARV is under $80K,

subtract $15K

If ARV is over $80K,

subtract 20% of the ARV

Subtract at least $5K for you –

$_____

(or whatever you want)

Equals the most you would offer =

(TOTAL) $_____,

Remember, you can always offer less. You may also have no clue as to the cost of repairs. You can get bids, ask the owner what he thinks it will cost, or come up with a ballpark figure. This doesn't have to be rocket science. You could get three bids and there could be a $20,000 difference.

One investor may think it needs $10K worth of work and another thinks it will be more like $23K. If you would rather work with percentages, you will find it depends a lot on the area and the prices. Here is an average percentage guide you can use:

Low-Income Areas – Offer 35 to 70% below ARV

Working Class Areas – Offer 25 to 40% below ARV

Middle-Income Areas – Offer 20 to 30% below ARV or 30% below $160,000 Equals $112,000

Let's see how using the percentage would work:

FOR EXAMPLE		
	ARV	$160,000
minus	repairs	$30,000
minus	profit for investor	$32,000
minus	your profit (what you want)	$10,000
equals the most you would offer		$88,000

	ARV	$160,000
minus	repairs	$30,000
minus	purchase price	$112,000
leaves profit for you and investor to split		$18,000

This is not a deal that would be appealing to the investor and would offer you very little, if any, profit!

As you can see, if there are lot of repairs, using percentages alone will not work. If there had been only 10K worth of work, here is how the numbers would have gone offering 30% below. This would be an easy deal to wholesale to an investor!

NEGOTIATING WITH THE SELLER

1 Introduce yourself

2 Find out if they are the seller

3 Ask, "Do you have few minutes to answer some questions?"

Now take a moment and explain a little about how you operate. You need to let the seller know how and why you buy. You need to let them know you buy one of two ways: cash or terms.

"When I buy with all CASH, it is at a discount. I will fix up the property and sell it on a new loan to a new owner. Often, this requires me to do a lot of repairs and bring it up to minimum housing codes. Or I buy the property with terms such as owner financing and that usually means I will keep it as a rental. I may even owner finance it for one of our potential homeowners that we currently have approved."

If you have their interest, continue to see if it's a real deal!

4. Where is the property located?

5. How much are you asking?

6. Do you own the property free and clear?

7. If YES, this is great because they can do whatever they want to do.

8. If NO, ask:

a. What is your Loan Balance?

b. How many years are left on the principal balance?

c. How much are the monthly payments? Does this include taxes and insurance (PITI)?

d. What is the least you will take as a down payment?

9. Roughly, how much do you think is needed to repair the property?

10. What is the lowest you will take, on a cash or a term basis? Stop and wait. (Remember, you have told them you are an investor who buys houses for cash to resell or for terms to hold for residual income). Let them think about it; see what they say.

11. Have you had any offers?

a. If so, what were they?

b. Why didn't you accept any?

12. How long have you been trying to sell?

Now, you pause. Wait and see how they respond to your conversation. Remember, if someone is not motivated now, that does not mean they will not be motivated later. So, we need to let them know if it is not going to work for us, they can call us later if they do not have any luck in selling.

Now end with this: "What will you do if you do not sell the property?"

This is a great way to end. It makes them really think, "What if?" However, if it looks positive, you will need to set up an appointment with them to look at the property

immediately and get a signed contract. Whatever you do, don't procrastinate; if you do, someone else will get there first and they will be the one making the money!

A useful tip when negotiating: Most of the time you should make both a cash offer and a terms offer at the same time. People love choices and it helps them see the difference in regards to the cash discount versus terms. It also lets them decide if it is really cash now that they need or getting closer to the full price offer that they want, which is only available if we can get owner financing.

CONTRACTS

Remember, these are SAMPLE contracts. It is recommended that you have your attorney review your contracts to at least come up with a good standard contract before you start preparing contracts.

To be a binding contract, it must be in writing. You can use contracts found in proprietary software or get one from your local Board of Realtors. You can also use a Letter of Intent, a one-page offer that is simple and helps you in negotiations when you are using a real estate agent and don't want to burn them out when making lots of offers at once. Make sure they are comfortable with it.

In order to be able to have the right to assign a contract, the buyer's name is listed as your name and/or assigns as the buyer. This gives you the right to assign the contract. Always put in your subject to clauses – give yourself a minimum of 10 business days. This is for your protection.

Closing should be a minimum of 30 days, preferably 45 to 60 days. If the seller feels this is too long, tell him it takes about 10 business days to get all the contractor bids completed. Tell them if it does not work for you, then you will back out of the contract within the 10-day inspection period so it doesn't tie up the property. Use your title company or lawyer to close. Always try to have your seller and your buyer pay all the closing costs.

Do not give a large deposit, even if the agent tells you to. $10 is preferable, but you may have to give $100. Never give the deposit to the seller. Always have the title company or your attorney hold the check.

Here's how it looks:

Assignment of Contract

First Contract

• Get a signed purchase contract

• Fax purchase contract to closing agent

• Start marketing for your new buyer

• Assign the contract Assignment Contract

• Fax assignment contract to closing agent

• Take backup offers until closed

Once closed... collect your check!

What Happens on the Day of Closing?

• New buyer comes to closing with all the money

• Seller comes to closing to sign and get his/her money

• You show up and get your check

Double Closing First Contract

• Get a signed purchase contract with you as the buyer

• Fax purchase contract to closing agent

• Start marketing for your new buyer

• Find new buyer, sign second purchase contract with you as the seller

Second Contract

• Fax second purchase contract to closing agent

• Take backup offers until closed Once closed... collect your check!

What Happens on the Day of Closing?

• New buyer comes to closing with all the money

• Seller comes to closing to sign and get his/her money

• You show up last and sign both the purchase contract with you as the buyer and the second purchase contract with you as the seller and collect your check.

WHY WHOLESALING?

Wholesaling is one of the quickest ways you can make money in real estate investing. And it can work for everyone. It is not necessary to have great people skills to negotiate a wholesale deal. If you lack confidence, putting money in your pocket quickly will certainly do a lot to build confidence.

You don't have to use any of your money or go out and get a loan. You don't have to spend a lot of time fixing up the property. And you can avoid holding costs. You will not have to worry that the property may not sell and you have to keep making those monthly payments. You don't have the risk that, as you rehab the home, you may run into major issues with electrical wiring or plumbing.

Potential wholesale properties are often very easy to locate. You will find them in low- to middle-income neighborhoods where there are distressed properties and more renters than owners. If you happen to live in a middle-income neighborhood where none of these types of properties exist, get out of the area. It will open your eyes. Drive 20 minutes out of some cities and you will find yourself in a totally different market. There are varying real estate prices even in close geographic areas. Look in the areas where the working class lives. You can do it!

In some areas, you will find that a four hundred thousand dollar home is a distressed property. You will see this all the time in California. Don't be discouraged. You can still wholesale four hundred thousand dollar houses! You may not do as many, but you can still make money from them. Just find the motivated seller with a distressed property or situation.

As your understanding of wholesaling grows, you will see that you can apply wholesale strategies to other real estate avenues such as pre-foreclosures. For example, you can wholesale a pre-foreclosure! However, you will find that HUD and VA will not allow you to put the house under contract with "and/or assigns" attached to it (additionally, many banks will not allow an assignment of contract).

Some investors will make an offer in the name of a trust and then assign their beneficial interest to the investor before closing. Be careful with HUD and VA foreclosures. You should never bid on the owner occupied ones unless you plan to LIVE in them. We are not saying planning on living there and later changing your mind. DO NOT BID if it is on an owner occupied list. Why do we stress this so much? Because doing otherwise can land you in jail. If the HUD and VA properties do not sell while on the owner-occupied list, they will be offered to all bidders. That is the time you can go in and make an offer through a HUD-certified agent.

When you cannot put the offer in your name and/or assigns, you can leave it out and do a double closing. This is very characteristic of what many investors will do. Remember, some banks will allow and/ or assigns. But you will find, for the most part, banks are not excited about and/or assigns.

Another caution is that when you are dealing with HUD and VA, you may find they have certain stringent requirements about the deposit and if you can get it back. Find out how the system works by asking a HUD- or VA -certified agent who specializes in this kind of property.

EXIT STRATEGIES

Some of you may decide that after you find the deal, you would rather go for the big money and fix it up and resell it. That's okay.

As you look at properties, you will be deciding what your exit strategy will be and that exit strategy can change based on the deal or your current situation.

Some properties you find you may never want to renovate. They may be so ugly, you think they should be torn down. But another investor may want it for the right price.

On others, you may decide you will try to wholesale the house, but if you can't make the money you want from wholesaling, you will buy the property yourself, fix it up, and make far more money than you planned. Then there will be the properties you want to do yourself right from the start, whether it is to fix the property up and sell it or hold on to it. You may exercise other techniques of real estate investing while holding the property. For example, you may rent it out and enjoy a positive cash flow along with the appreciation of the property. Or you might decide to do a lease option with the home, asking tomorrow's value but having cash flow today without the headache of being a landlord.

Understanding how to buy wholesale properties opens up a variety of exit strategies. The main thing you have to remember is you just need to DO IT!

Go out and look for wholesale properties. Make lots of offers and you will find a great avenue for quick cash.

At the close of this chapter are several sample forms and advertisements that can help you get started.

ASSIGNMENT

The following is a suggested assignment.

1 Target a low-income area

2 Know the value of homes in the area using the comps

3 Drive for dollars and market to find sellers

4 Get a real estate professional and title company on your power team

5 Make a lot of offers

6 Get a signed purchase contract with the seller in your name and/or assigns

7 Find your buyer

8 Sign an assignment of contract or a purchase contract with your buyer

9 Fax the documents to a title company or real estate attorney

10 Come to the closing and sign papers if doing a double closing

11 Collect your check!

12 Work on the 30-Day Plan of Action below

A 30-DAY PLAN
OF ACTION

The following is a suggested plan of action.

1. Set up shop

a. Get a separate phone and fax line

b. Get a d/b/a (doing business as - fictitious name)

c. Open a business checking account

d. Get business cards (can be simple... "I Buy Houses")

2. Locate tax assessor or county website

3. Market your business

a. Signs, flyers – get 1,000 printed up

b. Postcards for tracking vacant houses

c. Run ad: "I Buy Houses"

4. Join a real estate investment club

5. Choose an area to target

6. Find and train at least one real estate agent who understands this business and is willing to make multiple offers – possibly find at investor's club

7. Develop bird dog program, offer finder's fee

8. Drive for dollars at least 3 hours per week

9. Call the "I buy" ads

10. Find and put under contract at least one property you can assign or double close in the next 30 days

11. Be deal driven – don't care where you find the deals, just find good deals; that's all that matters

CHAPTER EIGHT

SECURING THE FINANCING

We have already discussed how you make your money in real estate when you buy and, therefore, the importance you need to place on buying right. To recap, you should never pay too much for the property. When you buy right, you are ensuring you get a great deal. And, as you already know, the key to finding a great deal is locating a motivated seller. But to be successful in real estate investing, you need to know not only how to find the motivated sellers and the great deals, but also how to find the money for those deals.

In fact, in real estate investing, what can make or break the deal is the financing. So you have probably already been asking the common question many students and investors ask: "Where do I get the money?" To finance your deals, you can use traditional lenders such as banks and mortgage companies. But if you don't have the best of credit or your debt-to-income ratio is too high, you will need to find alternative sources of money. In this chapter, we will discuss several creative financing options available to you, so no matter your situation or the transaction, you will have the resources you need to close the deal.

GETTING CREATIVE

The more creative you are as you finance your deals, the more successful you will be. A crucial element to creative real estate investing is how well you solve the problems of your sellers. Motivated sellers have a need, and as you satisfy this need, you create a win/ win situation. You can make a lot of money helping others solve their problems. And, as you learn different techniques and strategies, you will understand terms can sometimes be more significant than price or equity. You may have heard from many well-intentioned people that there is no such thing as a no money down deal. This can become discouraging, especially if you have heard this said by a professional in the business, such as a real estate agent or a mortgage broker. You may even hear some investors say you have to have money to buy real estate. But think of it this way: These skeptics have not used any creative financing or no money down techniques themselves, so they do not comprehend how you can own a property with no money down. Having said that, even though many investors have purchased real estate with no money down, creative financing does not always mean "no down payment." It usually refers to not using any of your own money. Instead, you want to use OPM, an acronym for Other People's Money. Using various strategies and methods, as well as OPM, will afford you almost limitless ways to fund your deals. Structuring a successful no money down transaction comes from understanding the necessary ingredients that will satisfy the seller's needs, while creating a great deal for you in the process.

WORKING WITH MORTGAGE BROKERS

As you begin to build your power team, you will realize a good mortgage broker is essential to your being able to obtain financing for each transaction. You are looking for a creative broker who works with investors regularly and has many financing programs available. Mortgage brokers tend to be more creative than bankers since they have several sources for funds and a variety of loan programs at their disposal. Sometimes, however, you may find a small hometown bank will be eager to help you in your investing. Some of these hometown banks offer portfolio loans, a loan the bank keeps in-house and doesn't sell to the secondary market. When a lender sells a loan, there are strict guidelines they have to follow. If you have a good relationship with your banker and they do portfolio loans, they can sometimes be more lenient. Otherwise, you will probably find more creative financing using a mortgage Some mortgage brokers have access to private funds that require no qualifying by the borrower. Equity in the house is their only concern. It's not the cost of the money that matters; it's the availability that counts. You need a mortgage broker whenever you are going to deal in short-term money, unless you plan to develop relationships with your own private lenders. Generally, the money these mortgage brokers will find for you comes from private individuals. The only consideration for one of these private loans is the Loan-to-Value (LTV) ratio. This short-term money is valuable to us as investors because you can do a loan on the value of the house, not what you paid for it. So if you buy right, you can borrow the money to both purchase the property and cover the costs to rehab it. You just factor these expenses into the cost of the loan. Again, private investors are usually only concerned about LTV ratio and the safety of their investment. Typically we call private money "hard money" and these private lenders are sometimes called hard moneylenders. A hard moneylender lends at a low LTV, usually 60 to 75% of the after-repair value (ARV). They charge a higher interest rate (could be 12 to 18%) and points (1 point = 1%). The points are based on the amount you borrow and can usually be built into the loan. The payments are typically interest-only payments with a balloon payment of the principal balance due in six months to one year. Sometimes there are no payments and interest accrues with a balloon payment of principal and interest in six months.

CALLING MORTG AGE BROKERS

To find mortgage brokers, see if you can get referrals from a real estate agent or another real estate investor. Otherwise, simply open your newspaper or phone book and call those who sound creative. You don't have to make an appointment and meet with the broker; you just need to make the phone call. It takes time out of your busy schedule to go and meet with a broker only to find he/she cannot help you, so start with calls. When you call mortgage brokers, you may come across someone who is rude and/or someone you are not comfortable working with. Politely tell them thank you very much and hang up. Some students take this personally and feel if they had more knowledge, the broker would have treated them differently. But after you start talking with several brokers, you will find this simply isn't true. Some will be rude or impersonal, but you will find many who will be very helpful. As you talk with these mortgage brokers, you will see they are eager to assist you in understanding what they can do for you. When calling mortgage brokers or bankers, you should never give them your Social Security Number. Every time they run a credit check, it lowers your score. Before you allow the broker to check your credit, you will want to make sure they can help you. If you know your score, go ahead and tell them what it is. Just don't give out your Social Security Number until you are sure this is the broker you want to work with. Once you have decided this is the broker you are going to work with, then it is okay to let them run your credit and do a loan application so you can know just how they can help you and how much you can qualify for in purchasing real estate.

Pre-qualified Vs. Pre-Approved

You may have been asked, particularly by a real estate agent, "Have you been pre-qualified?" or "Have you been preapproved?" You may have wondered what the difference is between the terms prequalified and pre-approved. When you get pre-qualified, the mortgage broker is looking at your income and debt to see how much you can afford to pay in a mortgage payment. Based on on this information, they can then tell you the maximum amount of financing you can get. They will give you a pre-qualification letter stating you are qualified for a loan of "X" amount of dollars. This is not a guarantee they will lend you the money. It is simply stating how much you can borrow subject to verification of employment and income, approval of your credit, and an appraisal. Some sellers, particularly banks selling properties or individuals who are selling in a market where buyers demand is high, require a letter of prequalification before you can submit an offer. With pre-approval, you are considered a step closer to getting the financing. Your income, credit, and employment information is carefully checked. This is still, not a guarantee for the loan. Other considerations such as the appraisal and title work will be factored in before you obtain the loan. However, with a preapproval letter, your offer to purchase will put you in a stronger position with the seller, as your ability to obtain financing appears more solid. Also, since the loan has been "approved," you should be able to close quickly. This can be very appealing to the seller.

QUESTIONS TO ASK MORTGAGE BROKERS

When you call, introduce yourself, "Hello my name is _____. I am looking to buy some properties and have a few questions. Do you have a few minutes?" If they say yes, then start asking questions. Remember not to give them your Social Security Number.

1. What is the most you will lend on a non-owner occupied property? What is the minimum amount? In some areas of the country, you can purchase properties for $15,000. If the minimum they will lend is $40,000, you would want to know this.

2. What is the most percentage-wise you will lend on owner occupied loans? What is the most for investor loans? We are talking percentage or LTV.

3. Is that amount (the amount they are willing to lend) based on appraised value or purchase price? Most of the time, they will say purchase price or whichever is less (meaning appraised value or purchase price, whichever is less). We like it when they say "appraised value," but it is harder for investors to find this kind of loan. But if you do find one who answers appraised value, you will ask him/her specific questions. In this case, give the broker this scenario: Take whatever percent-

age they told you they would lend, then take off the percentage sign and add thousands of dollars to become your purchase price. In other words, if they told you they would lend you 80%, your purchase price becomes $80,000, 90% - $90,000.00, 70% - $70,000.00. If they told you they would lend you 80%, say to them: "Let's assume I find a house that appraises for $100,000. But my purchase price is actually $80,000 Would you lend me $100,000?" If they say no, they're talking purchase price or whichever is less! If they say they would lend you $100,000, then you will go one step further. Take $10,000 off the purchase price no matter what number you're using. In this instance, we will drop the purchase price to $70,000. Then ask: "Suppose I get an even better deal on this house that appraises for $100,000. Instead of paying $80,000, my purchase price is $70,000! Would you lend me $100,000?" If they say yes, ask one more question: "Do you lend on the after-repair value?" After-repair value means the appraiser says this is what the property is worth fixed up and they look at that number rather than the as-is value.

The next list of questions is for everyone, whether they loan based on appraised value, purchase price, or whichever is less.

4. Do you allow the seller to take back a note? When a seller takes back a note, he is holding a second mortgage, possibly what would have been your down payment. This can be one way to get in with no money down. Some will say "yes," some will say "no," and others will say "yes, but..." The ones who say yes want money from you. They may do an 80-10-10, meaning 80% 1st mortgage, 10% seller

carry 2nd mortgage, and 10% out of your pocket. Or they may do an 80-15-5, with 5% from you. The brokers who say they do allow the seller to take back a note may still want money from you.

Verify just what they mean by asking:

"So if the seller were willing to take back a 2nd mortgage of 20%, you would give me an 80% 1st mortgage? Is that correct?"

You want to know now, not just before closing if they want money out of your pocket.

5. Do you do piggybacks? A piggyback is where the broker uses either the same lender, but two loans, or two different lenders. It is usually an 80% 1st mortgage and a 20% 2nd mortgage. That's 100% financing. The 80% 1st mortgage is usually at the normal investor interest rate. The 20% is typically higher; it could be as much as 10% interest. Not long ago, it was easy for an investor to get a piggyback, but now it is harder. But if you have not purchased a home, this is still commonly used for owner occupied homes.

6. Do you have any creative financing, private investors, or hard money? If they say they do, ask them what kind of creative financing they have. Can they get you in with no money down? Do they have access to a lot of hard money and work regularly with private investors? Also, ask about the terms of the private investors or hard moneylenders as they can vary from lender to lender.

7. Do you have any equity lenders? Equity lenders

lend a low L TV, usually anywhere from 60 to 70% of the appraised value. Typically, they are not as expensive (point and interest wise) as a hard money lender. The loan is usually a short-term loan of one to two years and there could be a prepayment penalty on the loan.

8. Do you offer any loans for fixing up the property? Sometimes they have rehab loans to fix up the property or construction loans where they lend you the money to buy the property and rehab it. Sometimes they have Title One loans and FHA 203K loans.

9. Do you have any non-conforming loans available, given the tight lending guidelines in place at the present time? While lending guidelines are currently hampered by constraints, money does seem to be loosening up at the time of this writing, so we are including some of the types of loans that have historically been available and encourage you to ask your mortgage broker about them. While they may not all be available in today's lending market, things change rapidly and a creative and knowledgeable lender will have some, if not all, of these loan products at their disposal.

Here are some examples of non-conforming loans and their description:

Stated income loans – You do not have to prove how much money you make. It originally started for business owners who take a lot of deductions.

No ratio loans – No debt-to-income ratio. They will verify employment and assets, but not your income. If you are self-employed, they need to see a two-year business license or verification from a CPA of two years employment.

NINA – No income or asset verification. They will check your credit and verify you have a job. They will not verify where you are getting your down payment. It can come from a third party! They don't care where the money comes from (cash advance, relative, etc).

No Doc – No documentation. This type of loan only requires verification of where you have lived for the last two years. No income, no assets, no employment. These loans have a little higher interest rate than conforming loans, but offer a lot more versatility to an investor.

10. Is the loan based on the property itself or do you look at my income? If you are buying income property, they will usually count 75% of the income. As long as your mortgage, taxes, and insurance are less than 75%, you should not have a lot of difficulty qualifying for the loan.

11. Up to how many units do you lend? Up to four is considered residential; five or more is considered commercial. Commercial loans will be different and you don't need to know how they work at this time. But if you do find a great commercial property later on, you will know which brokers to call back, including the commercial loan officer at the bank.

12. What is the interest rate? This will change from day to day, but it helps to have a ballpark number.

13. What kind of fees do you charge? When they talk

about points, remember one point equals one percent of the loan.

14. Do you allow the seller to pay the closing costs? How much do closing costs typically run? They will usually allow the seller to pay 3% of the purchase price in closing costs.

15. Do you allow some type of seller concession, such as a repair or decorating allowance? Usually they will allow the seller to give a repair or decorating allowance that will come out at closing. They usually allow a certain percentage. If they tell you 6%, ask if the seller pays the closing costs, is that 6% total, or 6% concession plus 3% closing cost, equaling a total of 9%? Often, they allow a maximum of 6% to be paid by the seller.

16. How long does it usually take to get an approval? How quickly can you close? You want to make sure you put a long enough timeframe in your contract. Usually make your closing date a little longer than the broker expects it to be.

17. What would you like to see in a loan package? Try to have everything they ask for to expedite the loan process.

18. If the seller were to put me on the deed, could I get a refinance loan instead of a purchase loan? Refinance is always based on appraised value. If we buy below the appraised value of the property, we can get in with no money down. Be sure to ask them if there is any "seasoning." Seasoning means you are required to have been on the deed for a period of time, usually six months to one

year.

SELLER FINANCING

What is seller financing? Seller financing simply means the seller is not getting all cash at closing. It may mean the seller receives no cash but will receive mortgage payments from you each month. They are the bank! They did not lend you the money; instead, they took a promissory note and secured that note with a mortgage.

Sometimes the seller will receive some cash at closing from the loan you received from the bank and the difference between the loan and the purchase price in payments as a second mortgage. For this to work, you will need to find a lender who allows the seller to carry some of the financing.

Seller financing is the best financing of all. You will find you save money by not having to pay fees associated with getting a loan, such as points and origination fees. Often, you can negotiate a better interest rate, especially when savings accounts in banks are receiving lower interest rates.

And with owner financing, you can easily negotiate certain terms in the mortgage that will benefit you. For example, you can put special clauses in your mortgage that will allow you to transfer a mortgage to another property (substitution of collateral clause) or allow you to obtain a new first mortgage (right to subordinate clause). There are no due on sale or balloon payment provisions in the mortgage if you do not put them there. Some sellers will actually do 100% financing. Always ask the seller if they will carry 100% of the financing. Worst-case scenario, they tell you no. But sometimes they will say yes!

When trying to get the seller to create 100% financing, you have to gain their trust. If they are concerned about no cash from you, you can help them feel more secure by giving something extra.

With any mortgage or deed of trust, there are two basic documents. The first is a promissory note given by the buyer to the seller acknowledging the debt as well as a promise to pay and the terms of the note. The other is a security instrument called a mortgage or deed of trust.

In the mortgage or deed of trust, the buyer who signed the promissory note pledges the property being financed as security (collateral) for the debt. The mortgage is a lien, not evidence of the debt. In essence, when a buyer signs the mortgage, he or she is saying, "If I do not perform according to to the terms of the note, then you can take back the property."

When there is no cash given as a down payment, the seller may be concerned that if the property was damaged, they could lose money. The property itself may not be able to satisfy the debt. If you give them something extra, like a lien on one of your other properties, they may feel more secure knowing the extra collateral will give them some cushion. The note stays the same; only the mortgage or deed of trust is changed.

Most of the time, however, you will have a seller who wants some cash in their pocket upfront. Now you have to find out what the needs of the seller are.

Does the seller need some cash right now? Or does the seller feels that if you have a vested interest in the property, you will take better care of it and make the monthly payments? In other words, is the seller just looking for security?

If the seller needs cash and wants a hefty down payment, maybe the seller could subordinate his position, allowing you to get a first mortgage with a lender and have the seller hold a second mortgage. See the example below.

FOR EXAMPLE,	
asking price	$100K
seller willing to carry	$80K mortgage
down payment	$20K
you offer	$100K
give seller	$40K from 1st mortgage loan from the bank
seller will carry	$60K 2nd mortgage

If the seller needs security, knowing that he received more money up front may help alleviate some of his fears. In this case, you may offer to give the seller more money and have him carry less.

See the example below.

FOR EXAMPLE,	
asking price	$100K
seller willing to carry	$80K mortgage
down payment	$20K
you offer	$100K
give seller	$60K 2nd mortgage
seller will carry	$40K from 1st mortgage loan from the bank

If the seller is not comfortable in holding a lien in the second position, then maybe you can give the seller even more cash and have a much lower mortgage. See the example below. If the seller is still concerned about holding a note in second position, you will need to try to find out what will work for the seller and still get you what you want. We will explore other options that may be more appealing to the seller shortly.

FOR EXAMPLE,	
asking price	$100K
seller willing to carry	$80K mortgage
down payment	$20K
you offer	$100K
give seller	$75K 2nd mortgage
seller will carry	$25K from 1st mortgage loan from the bank

Due-On-Sale Clause and Land Trusts

Sometimes the seller has a mortgage on the property, but they may still be willing to work with you on the financing. If the mortgage is assumable and does not require a new buyer to qualify, then you can assume the mortgage and ask the seller to carry a second mortgage for the difference between the purchase price and the assumable mortgage. But when the mortgage is not assumable or when qualification by a new buyer is required in order for an assumption to take place, there will be an acceleration clause in the mortgage that states if the property is sold, the lender has the right to demand payment of the remaining principal balance. This is sometimes referred to as the "due-on-sale clause." In other words, if the title is transferred, the bank may decide to "call the loan due."

Back in the '70s when interest rates began skyrocketing, people started having trouble selling their homes. So sellers had to get creative. They started letting more buyers assume their mortgages or they created wraparound mortgages. The banks wanted the money that had been locked into low interest loans to be available to lend at the higher market interest rates. The acceleration clause (a.k.a., due-on-sale clause) was a way of eliminating low interest loans and freeing up money to lend at the higher rates.

Wraparound Mortgages

Wraparound mortgages are an important tool in buying houses when there is an existing mortgage on the property. A wrap is a seller carry back loan that surrounds (or wraps) already existing financing. It enables the buyer to obtain financing without paying off the existing loan.

The buyer's mortgage and payments are based on the terms of the wrap, such as interest and timeframe, and have nothing to do with existing financing. The seller keeps the difference between what he or she receives from the buyer and the mortgage payment of the existing financing.

To illustrate, let's say you negotiate to purchase a house for $130,000. The seller is willing to do a wrap mortgage for the full purchase price at 10% interest amortized over 30 years. The seller's existing loan is based on an original loan of $80,000 at 7% interest amortized over 30 years. The seller has owned the property for 10 years.

This is how it looks:

• $130,000 at 10% interest amortized over 30 years = $1,140.84 per month

• $80,000 at 7% interest amortized over 30 years = $532.24 per month.

Each month, the seller will receive $608.60 more than his or her mortgage payment. At the end of 20 years, the seller will keep the full $1,140.84 per month until the principal is paid off in 10 years.

In essence, a wrap allows the buyer to take title to a property by combining a first mortgage and a second mortgage where the second mortgage wraps around the first. Sometimes it is called an all-inclusive mortgage (AIM) or an all-inclusive trust deed (AITD).

Land Contract, Contract for Deed, and Agreement for Deed

The terms land contract, contract for deed and agreement for deed essentially mean the same thing: a promise to pay. Until the debt is paid, the seller retains title and the buyer receives an equitable interest in the property.

The buyer does not become the titleholder until the terms of the contract are satisfied, at which time the seller actually deeds the property to the buyer.

A contract sale is handled by an escrow company that holds the Warranty Deed signed by the seller until the buyer satisfies the terms of the contract.

One benefit of using land contracts or contract for deed is they can be used as a tool to avoid the due-on-sale clause, since title does not transfer until the terms are satisfied. Another benefit is there are minimum closing costs involved because owner financing is used.

OTHER LOW OR NO MONEY DOWN TECHNIQUES

Assume First Mortg Age And Have The Seller Carry A Second

One no money down technique is to assume the first mortgage and have the seller carry a second. Often, there is a huge difference between what you have negotiated with the seller as a purchase price and the assumable loan he or she has. This difference can empty your pockets quickly or put the deal too far out of reach. Ask the owner to carry a second mortgage for the difference.

Owner takes back a note

Another technique is to have the owner take back a note for a short period of time, allowing you to get a refinance loan instead of a purchase loan. A refinance is based on the appraised value and not the purchase price, so if you are buying below appraised value, you can get into the property with no money down. It can have interest accruing and mortgage payments or no payments and a balloon. However, you need to use caution when using this technique. Ensure you have a lender who can refinance quickly without seasoning and one who will base that refinance on appraised value even though you have not owned the property for very long.

Split funding

With split funding, the investor offers a small amount of cash to close the deal, with the remaining amount due months later. No interest is paid and only one lump sum payment is due. Basically, it is a way of getting in with no down payment or with very little down and then having a balloon payment of the principal due later, such as in six months.

The term is negotiable, but enables the investor to fix up the property and have it sold or refinanced before the balloon is due. The advantage to the seller is that a distressed property gets fixed up and the seller gets his or her money no later than when the balloon payment comes due.

Balloon the down payment

This is similar to split funding, but you give no cash. Instead, you ask the seller if he or she will carry the note and wait six months or longer for the down payment. You will be making mortgage payments each month, which may relieve the owner of debt if it is a wrap mortgage or of management woes if the seller owns it free and clear. This can also solve problems the owner may have if they live out of state.

Additionally, this will give you time to come up with the money if you plan to sell the property and thus pay off the debt and pocket the difference. Or if you are planning on keeping the property, you can possibly use the extra money from the rents (your positive cash flow) to come up with the down payment, or you may decide to refinance.

Pay the down payment in installments

You can ask the seller to let you pay the down payment in terms. The payments can be made over several months or years. Of course, if you are keeping the property for income, you will want to make sure it still has cash flow.

Subordination

Subordination is simply moving a senior loan to junior position. It allows you to get a new mortgage, even though you already have seller financing in place. In other words, subordination occurs when the seller agrees to take back a second mortgage and allows you to get a first new mortgage on the property. IIt works best with properties carrying low or no mortgages.

Why are sellers willing to subordinate? You may find an extremely, motivated seller. Perhaps they have a distressed property they cannot sell. Or they may get more money from you with subordination than they would get if they sold the property "all cash" to some other buyer. Remember, the sales price can sometimes mean more to the seller than cash.

Substitution of collateral

Substitution of collateral simply means you are taking an existing mortgage on one property and you are transferring it to another. In other words, you are substituting the collateral from one property to another. This can work for a down payment or can be used to purchase the property. In using substitution of collateral to purchase the property, you will now own it free and clear. You can then refinance it, pulling cash out for future investing or to pay off the loan that was placed on an existing property you own.

Joint venture with the seller

Some deal types may not allow for this and it is recommended that you consult your local attorney for specific laws and regulations in your area.

Ask the seller to let you help sell his or her property and split the profit between you. If there is a lot of equity or you can force the appreciation by doing a little repair, you and the seller can make some good money. Make sure you have a contract that states how much the split is and the terms you have negotiated for your protection.

Joint venture with an investor

Let's say you find a phenomenal deal, but you are strapped for money. You could bring in another investor to be the money partner. Often, in the commercial arena, an investor will bring in several other investors to purchase high rises, etc.

Partners

When using partners, you need to have all your numbers worked out and the entire deal planned very carefully. It is customary to split the profit equally, but sometimes you may do a 40/60 or 30/70 deal.

How do you find a partner? Attend your local real estate investment group or advertise in the newspaper.

Important Note: When using a partner, be sure to consult with an attorney. It may not be in your best interest to create a partnership. Many people have been hurt as the result of a partner incurring litigation, and having judgments attached to them and their assets because of the partnership. It is usually best to keep them as a money partner where both of you are placed on the deed. This way, when the property is sold, you both will receive your portion of the profit.

Raise the price and lower the terms

To make seller financing work, particularly with no down payment, you can offer to pay more money than the seller is asking. This may appeal to a seller who is more concerned with price than the terms and doesn't really need the cash.

Lower the price and raise the interest rate

This is often used to appeal to an investor who wants a higher interest rate and sees the potential of making more money if the note is carried over a long term. This is beneficial to you because your interest payments are tax deductible, and if you do sell the property, you owe less because of the lower price (you have more equity in the property). Again, knowing the needs or desires of the seller can help you create the optimum win/win situation.

Assume the seller's obligations

Instead of giving cash for a down payment, you can assume the seller's financial obligations. If the seller has a payment they need to make, you could make the payment and count that as your down payment. Or maybe, you could take over a credit card bill and spread the down payment over several months or years.

Get a line of credit

There are many different types of lines of credit. You may have a strong portfolio with your bank and can get an unsecured line of credit.

Another line of credit is one that is secured. Possibly you have a large sum in the bank and you borrow against that amount. This may freeze up your account, but it can prove valuable in building a strong relationship with your bank for future lines of credit that won't be secured. It can also improve your credit as the bank reports your good payment history to credit bureaus.

Another secured line of credit may be taken on a property you own. This could be your personal residence, or it may be another investment property you own. It is usually called an equity loan and is based on the equity you have in the property.

For instance, if you own a property worth $100,000 and owe

$50,000, the lender may give you $30,000 in a line of credit, which becomes a second mortgage. You will then have the option of pulling out all of the $30,000 at once, or you will be given checks to use as needed.

The advantage of a line of credit is that if you need only $5,000 for a down payment or for repair costs and pull out just the $5,000, you will only pay interest on that $5,000. If you then pay the $5,000 back, you will have no interest accruing, but will still have access to up to $30,000 whenever you need it!

Trade for the down payment

Trade something you already own that has value for the down payment. You may have something of value the seller would happily take as a down payment. It could be something as simple as a boat or a vehicle. It may be a rundown property a motivated seller deeded to you. Finding the needs of your seller will allow you to find creative solutions to fund the deal.

Use equity on an existing property

You may own a property that has a lot of equity. Many investors will refinance that property and pull out the equity to be used as down payments or to pay cash for the next deal, and then refinance that property after it has been fixed up if they plan to keep it. Or they will sell the property and then use the excess proceeds to buy again.

Buy low and refinance to pull your cash out

If you have cash, you may want to buy low and refinance to pull out your cash. But if you want to go this route, remember that some lenders may require seasoning.

Over the years, lenders were hurt by unscrupulous investors who would purchase a property, do shabby repairs, and then sell the property for more than the value using an appraiser who overinflated the appraisal. So many lenders started requiring seasoning. You may still find some lenders who don't have an issue with seasoning, but before you pay cash, make sure you can refinance quickly if that is your plan.

Use hard money

Hard moneylenders are a critical element to you being able to have quick access to cash. Liquidity can make the difference between getting the deal and losing it. Quick closings can also help you negotiate much lower prices. They are also vital for an investor who does not have good credit.

Hard moneylenders usually base the loan on the property itself, not your creditworthiness. Because they lend at a low LTV, they have less risk. If you don't make the payments, they simply take the property and sell it.

As already discussed, we can find hard moneylenders through mortgage brokers, but there are other ways to find these private investors. For instance, you can check the courthouse for private note holders. If you consistently see a name that doesn't look like an institutional lender, you have probably found a hard moneylender. Don't be confused if the note holder is in the name of a Corporation or LL C. Most investors who lend money will use one of these entities.

You can also find hard moneylenders through your local real estate investment club and through other networking opportunities. For example, network with other investors you meet when attending auctions and calling the "I buy" ads in the newspaper. You may come across a hard moneylender or someone who can refer you to a good one.

Other sources for finding hard money include professionals associated with the real estate business. For example, accountants and CPAs have clients who are looking to invest their money. They may already have clients who hold one or more notes. Likewise, insurance agents have to put the lender on hazard insurance policies. If you know an agent, maybe they would look through their records to find the private lenders. Title companies and closing attorneys prepare closing documents for private moneylenders. Most should be able to give you at least one source for hard money.

You can also look in the newspaper for hard moneylenders. Often, you can find people wanting to lend money in the classified ads of the newspaper under the financial, business, or real estate section. Sometimes they may appear as "loan sharks." Remember, it is not the cost of the money, but the availability of the money that makes hard money so appealing. If you factor in all the costs of the loan and can still make money, why wouldn't you use a hard moneylender? Most investors who plan to do rehabs will use a hard moneylender.

As mentioned before, hard moneylenders are private investors. They lend at a much higher interest rate, as mentioned before, hard money lenders are private investors who lend at higher interest rates and typically charge points. Again, remember one point equals one percent of the loan amount.

You would want to pay a higher interest rate with lower points than a lower interest rate with high points. For example, if you were to get a loan at 18% interest and 2 points that you had for six months, your cost for the loan would be 1-1/2% per month X 6 months (equals 9% + 2 points = 11%). If you were to get a loan at 12% interest and 10 points for the same period of time, your cost for this loan would be 16% (1% per month X 6 months equals 6% + 10 points = 16%).

You may consider negotiating with the seller to pay the points. This could potentially save you money, but it really is the same as getting the seller to accept a lower purchase price. However, you will find that for some sellers, this is preferable to actually accepting a lower price. The reason is they may not want to tell family members they accepted the lower price, when in fact they would accept less money.

This is something you may want to explore as you negotiate with the seller. The benefit of having a higher price for you is that it may be easier to turn around and sell the property for more money if it appears the purchase price was higher. Most hard money loans are short-term loans of six months to one year. The investor wants to get in and out quickly. They make their money on the points and when this money is freed up, they can lend it out again. They also want less risk and a short period of time fits their risk tolerance. Nevertheless, you may want to ask them if there is a prepayment penalty if you pay the loan off early. There probably won't be, but it never hurts to ask.

Wanting to protect their interest, hard moneylenders will usually lend 60 to 75% of the after-repair value. They usually do their own drive-bys to ascertain the value of the property, but they may use someone else, an appraiser or someone they trust, to assess the ARV for them.

After you have established a good relationship with a hard moneylender and they feel you know what you are doing, some will put the money in your bank account within 24 hours. This will enable you to take advantage of foreclosure auctions and other deals that may need quick cash. And for those of you who may have trouble getting a loan through an institution because of credit issues, a hard moneylender can give you a pre-qualification letter, enabling you to make offers on bank owned properties and to sellers who insist on having a pre-qualification letter.

The bottom line is every investor should have at least one hard moneylender in their pocket!

Sell off part of the property

Sometimes you will buy a property that can be split into several useful parts. You can sell off part of the land or some of the houses and use the profit from that sale to make your down payment on another sale.

For example, let's say you are buying six houses at $25,000 each. You negotiate a 60-day close and you need 20% down. You sell two of the houses for $40,000 each. At the simultaneous closings, you make your down payment of

$30,000 from the profit you made from the sale of the two houses.

Blanket mortgage

A blanket loan covers more than one parcel or lot. It is usually used to finance subdivision developments. However, it can be used to finance the purchase of any kind of property. Blanket mortgages are used for multiple reasons. For example, some lenders have a minimum amount they are willing to lend. If the house you want to purchase is less than what they are willing to lend, you may want to combine one or more properties in a loan that blankets them.

The advantage of a blanket loan is that you usually pay less in closing costs (one closing for several properties).

The disadvantage is if you want to sell one of the properties. To do so, you will need the lender to release it (usually they will for a price) or you will need to refinance. It is imperative that you get a partial release clause put into the mortgage contract to protect yourself (consult with a lawyer). This clause permits the borrower to obtain a release of any one lot or parcel from the lien by repaying a certain amount of the loan. The lien will stay in place on the remaining properties.

Another reason you may want a blanket mortgage is because once you have multiple loans, it becomes harder to get a loan. By combining several properties you are purchasing, you will have less loans on the books.

Sometimes a lender will insist upon a blanket mortgage to reduce their risk. They lend you the money to purchase the property, but they want to attach the loan to the one purchased and a property you already own! Be careful. This is not a good loan for you.

When you are filling out loan applications, you need to be cautious. You have to show your debts, so those properties you have loans on will show up. But the properties you have purchased without institutional lending will not show up on your credit report. Even though they have equity, you may not want to list them as an asset. The lender may want to attach them into a blanket mortgage.

Making the seller your partner

Equity participation is when you make the seller your partner by giving them an interest in the property. For example, if your down payment was to be 20%, you can give the seller an equitable interest in the property of 20% instead of having to come up with the down payment. When you sell the property, the seller gets 20% of what the property sells for. To illustrate, if you purchased a property for $100,000, you would get a mortgage of $80,000 and give the seller a 20% interest in the property. Let's say that after two years, you sell the property for $150,000. The seller would receive $30,000 ($10,000 plus his initial $20,000) and you would profit $40,000! Win/win!

Equity part nership

This is similar to the equity participation made when the seller was your partner, but in this case, you make someone else your equity partner.

Let's say you are purchasing a property worth $180,000 for $120,000. Your lender requires $24,000 for a down payment.

You know your dad has been complaining about the low interest rate he has been receiving on his savings at the bank and that he is interested in doing some real estate investing. You sell him an equity share in the house. He has $12,000, so you give him a 10% share of the house.

You also have a couple of sisters who have expressed an interest in doing some investing. You ask them how much they can invest. an 8% share in the house. Your other sister who just got a bonus from work has $2,400 to invest. You give her a 2% share in the property. Now you have your $24,000 for the down payment and your family owns 20% of the house.

You purchase the house and sell it for $180,000. You will have $60,000 profit from the sale. Your dad gets $6,000 (plus his initial investment of $12,000); your sister who had an 8% share in the home receives $4,800 (plus her initial investment of $9,600); and the sister with the bonus has made $1,200 on her initial investment of $2,400. And you have made a handsome profit of $48,000!

Do you think your family might want to do this again? Do you think they may spread the word and you will have a lot more people wanting to own a share in the equity of a house?

Ask the agent to take back a note for his commission.

Some real estate agents may be willing to take back a note for their commission, particularly if they are having trouble selling the property. Most of them realize something is better than nothing. If their commission would be the down payment you need, then taking back a note could close the deal.

Also, if the owner does 100% financing, he or she may be unable to pay the agent because of lack of funds. You can always ask!

Closing strategies on cash flow properties

On income-producing properties, setting the closing date between the 3rd and 5th day of the month can help you produce the down payment you need.

At closing, you would get most of the rent for that month, plus the deposit and the last month's rent. Taxes are usually prorated and the real estate tax credit could also help with the down. But be aware that in some states, the deposit is held in escrow and you don't collect the last month's rent.

Find out what is applicable for you where you live. Sometimes the lender wants to see proof of funds and you have to bring money to the closing table, but you can put money back in your pocket afterward. With seller financing, you will not have to worry about proof of funds.

Create a note and sell it

There are many ways to create a note and many different types of notes. For example, when a seller carries the financing, a promissory note is created with the buyer promising to pay the debt and the terms of the note. A mortgage or deed of trust is created as a security instrument using the property as collateral for the debt. When a seller holds the "mortgage" or "takes back a note," the seller is holding a promissory note and a mortgage or deed of trust.

These notes and the security instrument can be sold to an investor. There are note buyers all over the country who buy notes on a daily basis. Most notes are sold at a discount, which is one of the ways a note buyer makes his or her money.

There are many factors that affect the value of the note. The primary factors are:

• The interest rate – The higher the interest rate, the more valuable the note, and the higher the yield.

• The credit of the borrower – The better the credit, the more the note buyer will pay for the note.

• Timeframe – The shorter the term, the more they will pay for the note. If it needs to be amortized over 30 years, then create a balloon in 10 years. Note buyers like to get in and out quickly. Since they buy at a discount, they make money when they buy.

• How old is the note? – They like notes to be "seasoned" one to two years. A seasoned note shows a payment history and provides less risk to the note buyer.

• LTV – How much is the loan to value? Note buyers want to see some equity in the property.

• What position is the note? – Typically, they want a note that is in first position.

• What kind of property, condition, and location? – They will take these factors into consideration.

These variables will affect how much the note is discounted and therefore the value of the note (what the note buyer ultimately will pay). Many investors will work with a seller to create a note that is sold at the same time the property is closed on and the seller gets cash at closing. This is a simultaneous close and even though it doesn't have any seasoning, this technique can be valuable to the investor buying the property.

You can get creative working with notes. For example, you could sell a "partial" note (selling part of the payments for your down payment). To illustrate, let's say you make an offer on a property for $150,000. The seller owns it free and clear and is willing to carry the financing with 20% down at 10% interest amortized over 30 years. You offer to give the seller the $30,000 cash down payment he wants if he is willing to give up the first 28 monthly payments. You show him how this will make him more money. Here is how you get the $30,000 for the down and convince the seller to carry the financing:

Create a $150,000 note at 10% interest = $1316.36 monthly payments. You are going to sell off the first 28 months of payments for $30,937.77. This will give the investor who purchases the note $36,858.08 – a yield of 15%! From the $30,937.77, you will give the seller the $30,000 down payment.

After 28 payments, the mortgage reverts back to the owner. At this time there is a principal balance of $147,916.97. The seller already collected $30,000 and still has 332 months of payments coming!

If you added the principal balance of $147,916.97 to the $30,000 down payment, the owner has already made $27,916.97 in addition to the remaining payments he will be receiving. Even if you sold the property or refinanced it at this point, the owner will have made $27,916.97 above the purchase price!

If you continue making mortgage payments, the owner will

make $263.27 more per month than if you were paying on a $120,000 note ($150,000 purchase price minus $30,000 down = $120,000 note at 10% interest = $1053.09 monthly payments). You have just created a win/win situation!

Make sure that when you sign the purchase contract, you put in the contingency: "Sale is subject to buyer selling 28 monthly payments at $1316.36 for a minimum of $30,000." Your lawyer can help you with contingencies. The note sale will take place simultaneously with the purchase of the property giving the seller the $30,000 down payment.

1031 Tax Exchange

In layman's terms, a 1031 Tax Exchange allows an investor to pull his profit from one or more real estate properties to purchase other property without it becoming a taxable event.

An exchange occurs when an investor buys and sells a property simultaneously to defer capital gains tax. Capital gains tax can be permanently deferred as long as an outright sale does not occur. The properties have to be like-kind. All real estate is considered to be like-minded. Qualifications of a 1031 Exchange include:

• Must use a qualified Intermediary (Exchanger) that is unrelated

• The seller must identify the property he or she plans to purchase within 45 days of closing

• The property must be purchased within 180 days of closing

• The replacement property has to be the same or more than the property being sold

• The replacement property must be held for a minimum of two years

There are many things you can do when you implement a 1031 Exchange. For example, other investors may sell several properties at once to purchase a large commercial building using a 1031 Exchange. Consult with a tax professional for assistance with 1031 Exchanges.

Grants

There are many federal, state, and city grants available depending on where you live and what you want to do. For example, the government offers, several grants for property improvements, and property development that is intended to help low-income families' or the elderly. And there are grants available for rehabilitating specific geographical areas.

Talk to bankers, real estate agents, and your city to see if they know of any grants available and contact your local housing authority to find out how government grant programs work. You should also network with investors who do rehabs or provide housing for the low-income population.

You'll also want to check with the federal government. You can go to the hud.gov website and look up the grants that are available there. HUD (Department of Housing and Urban Development) provides numerous grants for neighborhood revitalization. Additionally, the USDA (U.S. Department of Agriculture) provides loans and grants for rural multi-family housing for low-income individuals.

Try to locate a government grant and loan specialist to help you take advantage of the various grants available.

Options/straight options

An option is basically securing the right to purchase a property up to a certain time period for a specific price. There is usually consideration money given that can be non-refundable. You are paying for the right to tie up the property for a period of time for an agreed upon price. The seller cannot sell the property to anyone else during this time. You are not obligated to purchase the property; you just have the right to purchase it for a certain period of time. Sometimes this is called a straight option.

Straight options are commonly used by developers purchasing raw ground and by those investing in commercial properties. These developers and investors don't want to purchase a property only to find out that after they have run tests and feasibility studies, they cannot build on the property or that it is not suited for what they want to do. Sometimes they have to get zoning changes. At the same time, they don't want to spend all this time and money doing their due diligence only to find out the owner sold the property to someone else.

When it comes to houses, most people only think of lease option. But you can sometimes secure a straight option on a house and assign the option for a fee. Sometimes you will find a motivated seller who has not been able to sell the home. You know it is because the seller lacks the marketing skills and you feel you could sell this property quickly. Using an option would allow you to do just that.

Sandwich lease options

A sandwich lease option is where you buy with a lease option and then sell with a lease option. You are essentially sandwiched between two lease options.

Many investors like the sandwich lease option because you can usually get in with minimal cash (usually $100) and receive from your tenant/buyer 3 to 5% of the purchase price in option consideration money. At the same time, you can have positive cash flow.

The properties involved in lease options are usually nice homes in great neighborhoods. We will learn more about lease options in the next chapter. Be sure to look into the laws of your state regarding lease options.

Assignment of contract

We discussed assignment of contracts in our chapter on wholesaling, but, as a reminder, with an assignment of contract, you never purchase the property. You get the property under contract and either assign the contract or do a double closing. This is quick money with limited risk. You don't have to get a loan or rehab the property because you are not purchasing the property. You find a great deal and wholesale it to another investor who does all the work.

Review

There are probably a thousand and one ways to creatively purchase real estate. But the first step in creative financing is solving the problems of your motivated seller.

Become a problem solver! This is an essential component in real estate investing. Think creatively as you attempt to satisfy the needs of your seller.

Strive to produce a win/win situation at every opportunity. Sellers will work with you if they feel you can satisfy their needs and help them with their problem. Be creative.

DISCLAIMER

Disclaimer All the material contained in this book is provided for educational and informational purposes only. No responsibility can be taken for any results or outcomes resulting from the use of this material. While every attempt has been made to provide information that is both accurate and effective, the author does not assume any responsibility for the accuracy or use/mis-use of this information.